FARM
to
TABLE
Cookbook

Publications International, Ltd.

Art throughout and photographs on front cover (top left and right), back cover (middle) and pages 169, 173, 181, 185 and 187 copyright © Shutterstock.com.

Pictured on the front cover *(clockwise from top left):* Mediterranean Roasted Vegetables *(page 102),* Apple-Walnut Salad with Honey Vinaigrette *(page 25)* and Honey Lemon Garlic Chicken *(page 92).*

Pictured on the back cover *(top to bottom):* Cherry and Cheese Panini *(page 57),* Lemon Curd *(page 168)* and Oatmeal Porridge with Berry Compote *(page 5).*

ISBN: 978-1-64558-870-2

Manufactured in China.

8 7 6 5 4 3 2 1

Microwave Cooking: Microwave ovens vary in wattage. Use the cooking times as guidelines and check for doneness before adding more time.

WARNING: Food preparation, baking and cooking involve inherent dangers: misuse of electric products, sharp electric tools, boiling water, hot stoves, allergic reactions, foodborne illnesses and the like, pose numerous potential risks. Publications International, Ltd. (PIL) assumes no responsibility or liability for any damages you may experience as a result of following recipes, instructions, tips or advice in this publication.

While we hope this publication helps you find new ways to eat delicious foods, you may not always achieve the results desired due to variations in ingredients, cooking temperatures, typos, errors, omissions or individual cooking abilities.

Let's get social!
 @Publications_International
@PublicationsInternational
www.pilbooks.com

CONTENTS

BREAKFAST

OATMEAL PORRIDGE *with* BERRY COMPOTE

Makes 4 servings

- **4 cups plus 1 tablespoon water, divided**
- **½ teaspoon salt**
- **1 cup steel-cut oats**
- **½ teaspoon ground cinnamon**
- **⅓ cup half-and-half or milk**
- **¼ cup packed brown sugar**
- **1 cup fresh strawberries, hulled and quartered**
- **1 cup fresh blackberries**
- **1 cup fresh blueberries**
- **3 tablespoons granulated sugar**

1 Bring 4 cups water and salt to a boil in medium saucepan over medium-high heat. Whisk in oats and cinnamon. Reduce heat to medium; simmer, uncovered, about 40 minutes or until water is absorbed and oats are tender. Remove from heat; stir in half-and-half and brown sugar.

2 Meanwhile, combine strawberries, blackberries, blueberries, granulated sugar and remaining 1 tablespoon water in small saucepan; bring to a simmer over medium heat. Cook 8 to 9 minutes or until berries are tender but still hold their shape, stirring occasionally.

3 Divide porridge among four bowls; top with berry compote.

COUNTRY FRENCH EGGS

Makes 6 servings

- 6 **hard-cooked eggs, peeled and sliced in half lengthwise**
- 2 **tablespoons milk**
- 1 **tablespoon minced fresh tarragon** *or* **1 teaspoon dried tarragon**
- 1 **clove garlic, minced**
- ⅛ **teaspoon plus pinch of salt, divided**
- ⅛ **teaspoon plus pinch of black pepper, divided**
- 2 **teaspoons Dijon mustard**
- 2 **teaspoons tarragon vinegar or white wine vinegar**
- 1 **teaspoon honey**
- 1 **tablespoon olive oil**
- 1 **tablespoon butter**

1 Remove yolks from egg whites. Mash yolks in small bowl. Add milk, minced tarragon, garlic, ⅛ teaspoon salt and ⅛ teaspoon pepper; mix well. Reserve 2 tablespoons yolk mixture. Fill egg whites with remaining yolk mixture, patting firmly into each egg.

2 For sauce, add mustard, vinegar, honey, dash salt and dash pepper to reserved yolk mixture. Whisk in oil in thin steady stream.

3 Heat butter in large skillet over medium-low heat. Place egg halves, yolk side down, in skillet; cook 2 to 3 minutes or until yolk mixture is slightly golden. *Do not overcook.*

4 Pour sauce onto serving plates; top with eggs.

NOTE: For perfect hard-cooked eggs, bring a medium saucepan of water to a boil over high heat. Gently add eggs with slotted spoon. Reduce heat to medium to maintain a simmer; cook 12 minutes. Meanwhile, prepare an ice bath. Drain eggs and place in ice bath; cool at least 10 minutes.

CARAMELIZED BACON

Makes 4 to 6 servings

12 slices (about 12 ounces) applewood-smoked bacon

½ cup packed brown sugar

2 tablespoons water

¼ to ½ teaspoon ground red pepper

1 Preheat oven to 375°F. Line large rimmed baking sheet with foil. Spray wire rack with nonstick cooking spray; place on prepared baking sheet.

2 Cut bacon in half crosswise, if desired; arrange in single layer on prepared wire rack. Combine brown sugar, water and red pepper in small bowl; mix well. Brush generously over bacon.

3 Bake 20 to 25 minutes or until bacon is well browned. Immediately remove to serving platter; cool completely.

NOTE: Bacon can be prepared up to 3 days ahead. Store it in the refrigerator between sheets of waxed paper in a resealable food storage bag. Let stand at room temperature at least 30 minutes before serving.

BLUEBERRY PANCAKES

Makes 10 to 12 pancakes

**2 tablespoons plus
2 teaspoons butter**

1¼ cups milk

1 egg, beaten

1¼ cups all-purpose flour

½ cup fresh blueberries

¼ cup packed brown sugar

1 tablespoon baking powder

½ teaspoon salt

**Powdered sugar or maple
syrup**

1 Melt butter in large skillet or griddle over medium heat. Pour into medium bowl, leaving thin film of butter on skillet. Add milk and egg to butter; whisk until well blended.

2 Combine flour, blueberries, brown sugar, baking powder and salt in large bowl; mix well. Stir in milk mixture just until moistened.

3 Heat same skillet over medium heat. Pour ¼ cup batter into skillet for each pancake. Cook 2 to 3 minutes or until edges look dull and bubbles begin to form on surface. Turn; cook until lightly browned on both sides. Dust with powdered sugar.

APPLE CRÊPES

Makes about 14 crêpes

1 **cup all-purpose flour**

¼ **teaspoon salt**

¼ **teaspoon ground nutmeg**

1 **cup half-and-half or milk**

5 **tablespoons butter, melted, divided**

½ **teaspoon vanilla**

3 **eggs**

5 **Granny Smith apples, peeled and cut into ¾-inch slices**

¼ **cup dried cranberries**

1 **tablespoon sugar**

1 **teaspoon ground cinnamon**

1 Whisk flour, salt and nutmeg in medium bowl. Gradually whisk in half-and-half until smooth. Add 2 tablespoons butter and vanilla. Whisk in eggs, one at a time, until batter is smooth and the consistency of heavy cream.

2 Combine apples, cranberries, sugar and cinnamon in large bowl; toss to combine. Heat 2 tablespoons butter in large nonstick skillet over medium heat. Add apple mixture; cook and stir 5 minutes or until apples are softened. Keep warm.

3 Heat 8- or 9-inch nonstick skillet over medium heat. Brush lightly with remaining 1 tablespoon butter. Pour about ¼ cup batter into center of skillet; swirl to coat with batter. Cook 1 minute or until crêpe is dull on top and edges are dry. Turn and cook 30 seconds. Remove to plate and repeat with remaining crêpes.

4 Fill crêpes with apple mixture; serve immediately.

TIP: Freeze any leftover unfilled crêpes between sheets of waxed paper in a large resealable food storage bag for future use.

PEPPERY SKILLET POTATOES

Makes 4 servings

2 **tablespoons olive oil**

4 **red potatoes, cut into thin wedges**

½ **cup chopped onion**

2 **tablespoons lemon pepper**

½ **teaspoon salt**

Chopped fresh parsley (optional)

1 Heat oil in large skillet over medium heat. Add potatoes, onion, lemon pepper and salt; stir to coat. Cover and cook 25 to 30 minutes or until potatoes are tender and browned, turning occasionally.

2 Sprinkle with parsley just before serving, if desired.

KALE FRITTATA *with* BACON

Makes 4 to 6 servings

2 **teaspoons olive oil**

1 **small onion, chopped**

3 **slices bacon, chopped**

4 **cups coarsely chopped stemmed kale**

2 **cloves garlic, minced**

8 **eggs**

¼ **teaspoon salt**

¼ **teaspoon black pepper**

4 **ounces crumbled goat cheese**

1 Heat oil in large ovenproof skillet over medium heat. Add onion and bacon; cook and stir 6 to 8 minutes or until onion is golden brown.

2 Add kale and garlic; cook and stir 3 to 5 minutes or until kale is wilted. Evenly spread mixture to cover bottom of skillet.

3 Meanwhile, preheat broiler. Whisk eggs, salt and pepper in small bowl until well blended. Pour evenly over kale mixture; sprinkle evenly with cheese. Cover and cook 6 to 7 minutes or until almost set.

4 Broil, uncovered, 2 to 3 minutes or until golden brown and set. Let stand 5 minutes; cut into wedges to serve.

RASPBERRIES *and* CREAM STUFFED FRENCH TOAST

Makes 4 servings

6 ounces cream cheese, softened

3 tablespoons powdered sugar, plus additional for garnish

1 teaspoon ground cinnamon

¼ teaspoon ground nutmeg

8 slices sandwich bread

1½ cups fresh raspberries

⅔ cup milk

3 eggs, beaten

2 tablespoons maple syrup

1 teaspoon vanilla

2 tablespoons butter

1 Preheat oven to 350°F.

2 Combine cream cheese, 3 tablespoons powdered sugar, cinnamon and nutmeg in small bowl; mix well. Spread evenly onto one side of each slice of bread. Sprinkle raspberries over half of bread slices; close sandwiches, pressing down gently to flatten.

3 Whisk milk, eggs, maple syrup and vanilla in baking dish. Add sandwiches; turn to coat. Let stand 5 minutes or until fully soaked. Remove sandwiches, letting excess egg mixture drip back into dish.

4 Melt 1 tablespoon butter in large skillet over medium heat. Cook half of sandwiches 3 to 4 minutes per side or until golden brown. Place on baking sheet. Repeat with remaining butter and sandwiches.

5 Bake 10 minutes or until bread is crisp and sandwiches are heated through. Slice sandwiches and sprinkle with additional powdered sugar, if desired.

CHILE-CORN QUICHE

Makes 6 servings

Pie Pastry for Single Crust Pie (page 159)

1 **cup corn**

1 **can (4 ounces) diced mild green chiles, drained**

¼ **cup thinly sliced green onions**

1 **cup (4 ounces) shredded Monterey Jack cheese**

1½ **cups half-and-half**

3 **eggs**

½ **teaspoon salt**

½ **teaspoon ground cumin**

1 Prepare pie pastry. Roll out pastry into 11-inch circle on lightly floured surface. Line 9-inch pie plate with pastry; trim and flute edge.

2 Preheat oven to 450°F. Line pastry with foil and fill with dried beans or rice. Bake 10 minutes. Remove foil and beans. Bake 5 minutes or until lightly browned. Cool. *Reduce oven temperature to 375°F.*

3 Combine corn, chiles and green onions in small bowl. Spoon into crust; top with cheese. Whisk half-and-half, eggs, salt and cumin in medium bowl. Pour over cheese.

4 Bake 35 to 45 minutes or until filling is puffed and knife inserted into center comes out clean. Let stand 10 minutes before serving.

BAKED PUMPKIN OATMEAL

Makes 6 servings

2 cups old-fashioned oats

½ cup dried cranberries

1 teaspoon pumpkin pie spice

½ teaspoon salt

½ teaspoon baking powder

2 cups milk

1 cup canned pumpkin

2 eggs

⅓ cup packed brown sugar

1 teaspoon vanilla

Maple syrup

Chopped pecans (optional)

1 Preheat oven to 350°F. Spray 8-inch square baking dish with nonstick cooking spray.

2 Spread oats on ungreased baking sheet. Bake about 10 minutes or until fragrant and lightly browned, stirring occasionally. Pour into medium bowl; let cool slightly. Add cranberries, pumpkin pie spice, salt and baking powder; mix well.

3 Whisk milk, pumpkin, eggs, brown sugar and vanilla in large bowl until well blended. Add oat mixture; stir until well blended. Pour into prepared baking dish.

4 Bake about 45 minutes or until set and knife inserted into center comes out almost clean. Serve warm with maple syrup and pecans, if desired.

SALADS

APPLE-WALNUT SALAD *with* HONEY VINAIGRETTE

Makes 4 servings

¼ **cup chopped walnuts**

1 **tablespoon white wine vinegar**

2 **teaspoons olive oil**

2 **teaspoons honey**

¼ **teaspoon salt**

⅛ **teaspoon black pepper**

1 **large head Bibb lettuce, separated into leaves**

1 **small Red Delicious or other red apple, thinly sliced**

1 **small Granny Smith apple, thinly sliced**

1 **small red onion, thinly sliced (optional)**

¼ **cup crumbled blue cheese**

1 Place walnuts in small skillet over medium heat. Cook and stir 5 minutes or until fragrant and lightly toasted. Transfer to plate to cool.

2 Whisk vinegar, oil, honey, salt and pepper in small bowl until well blended.

3 Divide lettuce and apples evenly among four plates; top with onion, if desired. Drizzle dressing evenly over each salad; top with walnuts and cheese.

CRUNCHY JICAMA, RADISH *and* MELON SALAD

Makes 8 servings

3 cups julienned jicama

3 cups cubed watermelon

2 cups cubed cantaloupe

1 cup thinly sliced radishes

3 tablespoons chopped fresh cilantro

2 tablespoons olive oil

2 tablespoons fresh lime juice

1 tablespoon fresh orange juice

1 tablespoon cider vinegar

1 tablespoon honey

½ teaspoon salt

1 Combine jicama, watermelon, cantaloupe and radishes in large bowl; gently mix.

2 Whisk cilantro, oil, lime juice, orange juice, vinegar, honey and salt in small bowl until smooth and well blended. Add to salad; gently toss to coat evenly. Serve immediately.

BEET *and* BLUE SALAD
Makes 4 servings

1 package (6 ounces) baby spinach

1 cup sliced cooked beets

½ cup diced red onion

½ cup shredded carrots

¼ cup balsamic vinegar

2 tablespoons canola oil

2 tablespoons maple syrup

¼ teaspoon salt

⅛ teaspoon red pepper flakes

¼ cup crumbled blue cheese

1 Divide spinach among four salad plates. Top with beets, onion and carrots.

2 Whisk vinegar, oil, maple syrup, salt and red pepper flakes in small bowl until smooth and well blended. Drizzle dressing over salad. Sprinkle with cheese.

ORZO SALAD *with* ZUCCHINI *and* FETA

Makes 4 servings

½ **cup uncooked orzo**

1 **tablespoon plus 1 teaspoon olive oil, divided**

1 **tablespoon fresh lemon juice**

½ **teaspoon salt**

⅛ **teaspoon black pepper**

1 **cup coarsely chopped zucchini**

½ **cup finely chopped fresh Italian parsley**

⅓ **cup thinly sliced radishes**

⅓ **cup crumbled feta cheese**

2 **tablespoons thinly sliced green onion**

1 Cook orzo in medium saucepan of salted boiling water according to package directions for al dente. Drain and rinse under cold water; transfer to large bowl.

2 Meanwhile, whisk 1 tablespoon oil, lemon juice, salt and pepper in small bowl.

3 Heat remaining 1 teaspoon oil in small skillet over medium heat. Add zucchini; cook and stir 2 to 3 minutes or until softened. Add to orzo. Stir in parsley, radishes, cheese and green onion. Drizzle dressing over salad; toss gently to blend.

GRILLED STONE FRUIT SALAD

Makes 4 servings

2 **tablespoons fresh orange juice**

1 **tablespoon fresh lemon juice**

2 **teaspoons canola oil**

1 **teaspoon honey**

½ **teaspoon Dijon mustard**

1 **tablespoon finely chopped fresh mint**

1 **peach, halved and pitted**

1 **nectarine, halved and pitted**

1 **plum, halved and pitted**

4 **cups mixed baby greens**

½ **cup crumbled goat cheese**

1 Prepare grill for direct cooking over medium-high heat. Spray grid with nonstick cooking spray.

2 Whisk orange juice, lemon juice, oil, honey and mustard in small bowl until well blended. Stir in mint.

3 Brush cut sides of fruit with some of orange juice mixture. Set remaining dressing aside. Grill fruit, cut sides down, covered, 2 to 3 minutes. Turn; grill 2 to 3 minutes or until fruit begins to soften. Transfer to plate; cool slightly. Cut into wedges when cool enough to handle.

4 Arrange mixed greens on four serving plates. Top with fruit and cheese and drizzle with remaining dressing. Serve immediately.

HOT *and* SPICY FRUIT SALAD
Makes 6 servings

⅓ cup fresh orange juice

3 tablespoons fresh lime juice

3 tablespoons minced fresh mint, basil or cilantro

2 jalapeño peppers, seeded and minced

1 tablespoon honey

½ small honeydew melon, cubed

1 ripe large papaya, peeled, seeded and cubed

1 pint fresh strawberries, stemmed and halved

1 cup pineapple chunks

1 Whisk orange juice, lime juice, mint, jalapeños and honey in small bowl until well blended.

2 Combine melon, papaya, strawberries and pineapple in large bowl. Pour orange juice mixture over fruit; toss gently to coat.

3 Serve immediately or cover and refrigerate up to 3 hours.

GREEK-STYLE CUCUMBER SALAD

Makes 4 servings

1 cucumber, peeled and diced

¼ cup chopped green onions

1 teaspoon minced fresh dill

1 clove garlic, minced

1 cup sour cream

½ teaspoon salt

¼ teaspoon black pepper

⅛ teaspoon ground cumin

Fresh lemon juice (optional)

1 Combine cucumber, green onions, dill and garlic in medium bowl.

2 Combine sour cream, salt, pepper and cumin in small bowl; stir until blended. Add to cucumber mixture; stir until well blended. Sprinkle with lemon juice to taste, if desired.

SPRING GREENS *with* BLUEBERRIES, WALNUTS *and* FETA CHEESE

Makes 4 servings

1 **tablespoon canola oil**

1 **tablespoon white wine vinegar or sherry vinegar**

2 **teaspoons Dijon mustard**

½ **teaspoon salt**

½ **teaspoon black pepper**

5 **cups mixed spring greens (5 ounces)**

1 **cup fresh blueberries**

½ **cup crumbled feta cheese**

¼ **cup chopped walnuts or pecans, toasted***

*To toast nuts, place in small nonstick skillet. Cook over medium-low heat about 5 minutes or until nuts begin to brown, stirring frequently. Immediately transfer to plate to cool.

1 Whisk oil, vinegar, mustard, salt and pepper in large bowl until well blended.

2 Add greens and blueberries; toss gently to coat. Top with cheese and walnuts. Serve immediately.

SOUPS

CORN CHOWDER

Makes 6 servings

1 tablespoon butter

1 red bell pepper, diced

1 medium onion, diced

1 stalk celery, diced

2 cans (about 14 ounces each) vegetable broth

3½ cups corn

3 small potatoes, peeled and cut into ½-inch pieces

½ teaspoon salt

½ teaspoon black pepper

¼ teaspoon ground coriander

½ cup whipping cream

8 slices bacon, crisp-cooked and crumbled (optional)

1 Melt butter in large saucepan over medium-high heat. Add bell pepper, onion and celery; cook 5 to 7 minutes or until vegetables are softened, stirring occasionally.

2 Add broth, corn, potatoes, salt, black pepper and coriander; bring to a boil. Reduce heat to low; cover and simmer 30 minutes or until vegetables are very tender.

3 Partially mash soup mixture with potato masher to thicken. Stir in cream; cook over medium heat until hot. Adjust seasonings. Garnish with bacon.

PASTA FAGIOLI SOUP

Makes 4 to 6 servings

1 tablespoon olive oil

1 onion, chopped

2 zucchini, quartered
   lengthwise and sliced

1½ teaspoons minced garlic

2 cans (about 14 ounces each)
   vegetable broth

1 can (about 15 ounces) Great
   Northern beans, rinsed
   and drained

1 can (about 14 ounces) diced
   tomatoes

1 teaspoon salt

½ teaspoon dried basil

½ teaspoon dried oregano

½ cup uncooked tubetti,
   ditalini or small shell pasta

   Croutons and shredded
   Asiago or Romano cheese

1 Heat oil in large saucepan over medium-high heat. Add onion, zucchini and garlic; cook and stir 3 minutes or until zucchini is softened.

2 Add broth, beans, tomatoes, salt, basil and oregano; bring to a boil. Add pasta; cook 10 minutes or until pasta is tender. Serve with croutons and cheese.

TIP: This recipe can also be cooked in a slow cooker. Combine broth, beans, tomatoes, zucchini, oil, garlic, salt, basil and oregano in slow cooker; mix well. Cover; cook on LOW 3 to 4 hours. Stir in pasta. Cover; cook on LOW 1 hour or until pasta is tender. Note that only small pasta varieties like tubetti, ditalini or small shell-shaped pasta should be used in the slow cooker (the low heat won't allow larger pasta shapes to cook completely).

BUTTERNUT BISQUE
Makes 6 servings

1 **tablespoon butter**

1 **large onion, chopped**

1 **medium butternut squash
   (about 1½ pounds), peeled
   and cut into ½-inch pieces**

2 **cans (about 14 ounces each)
   vegetable broth, divided**

½ **teaspoon ground nutmeg**

⅛ **teaspoon white pepper**

   **Plain yogurt or sour cream
   and chopped chives**

1 Melt butter in large saucepan over medium heat. Add onion; cook and stir 3 minutes. Add squash and one can of broth; bring to a boil over high heat. Reduce heat to low; cover and simmer 20 minutes or until squash is very tender.

2 Purée soup in batches in blender, returning blended soup to saucepan after each batch. (Or use immersion blender.) Add remaining can of broth, nutmeg and pepper. Simmer, uncovered, 5 minutes or until heated through, stirring occasionally.

3 Ladle soup into bowls; serve with yogurt and chives.

FARMERS' MARKET GRILLED CHOWDER

Makes 4 servings

1 **ear corn**

1 **large potato**

1 **small zucchini, halved lengthwise**

1 **tablespoon vegetables oil**

1 **tablespoon butter**

½ **cup chopped onion**

2 **tablespoons all-purpose flour**

½ **teaspoon salt**

½ **teaspoon dried thyme**

⅛ **teaspoon white pepper**

1 **cup vegetable broth or wheat beer**

1 **cup milk**

½ **cup (2 ounces) shredded sharp Cheddar cheese**

1 Prepare grill for direct cooking. Remove husks and silk from corn. Cut potato in half lengthwise. Grill corn and potato, covered, over medium-high heat 20 minutes or until tender, turning once. Cut kernels from cob into large bowl. Cut potato into cubes; add to corn.

2 Brush zucchini with oil. Grill, uncovered, 4 minutes or until tender, turning once. Slice crosswise and add to bowl with vegetables.

3 Melt butter in large saucepan over medium heat. Add onion; cook and stir 5 minutes or until tender. Stir in flour, salt, thyme and pepper; cook and stir 1 minute.

4 Stir broth and milk into flour mixture. Bring to a boil. Reduce heat to medium-low; simmer 1 minute. Stir in vegetables and cheese. Simmer until cheese is melted and soup is heated through, stirring constantly.

MINESTRONE *with* BARLEY

Makes 4 servings

2 teaspoons olive oil

1 red onion, chopped

1 carrot, diced

1 zucchini, diced

1 stalk celery, diced

1 clove garlic, minced

2 cups vegetable broth

1 can (about 14 ounces) fire-roasted diced tomatoes

1 cup cooked pearl barley

¼ cup chopped fresh Italian parsley

1 teaspoon dried oregano

½ teaspoon salt

½ teaspoon black pepper

Grated Parmesan cheese

1 Heat oil in large saucepan over medium-high heat. Add onion, carrot, zucchini, celery and garlic; cook and stir 7 minutes.

2 Add broth, tomatoes, barley, parsley, oregano, salt and pepper to saucepan. Bring to a boil over high heat. Reduce heat to medium; cover and cook 15 to 20 minutes or until vegetables are tender and soup is thickened.

3 Ladle soup into bowls; top each serving with cheese.

CHUNKY TOMATO-BASIL SOUP

Makes 6 servings

2 tablespoons olive oil

1 cup chopped onion

2 cloves garlic, minced

5 cups peeled, seeded and chopped fresh tomatoes, divided

1 can (6 ounces) tomato paste

¼ teaspoon salt

½ teaspoon dried marjoram

¼ teaspoon black pepper

4 cups vegetable broth

3 tablespoons chopped fresh basil *or* 1½ teaspoons dried basil*

If using dried basil, add it in step 2 with the tomato paste.

1 Heat oil in large saucepan over medium heat. Add onion and garlic; cover and cook 7 minutes or until tender, stirring occasionally.

2 Stir in 4 cups tomatoes, tomato paste, salt, marjoram and pepper until well blended. Stir in broth. Bring to a boil. Reduce heat to low; cover and simmer 30 minutes. Stir in basil.

3 Purée soup in batches in blender or food processor (or use immersion blender). Return soup to saucepan. Stir in remaining 1 cup tomatoes. Cook over medium heat until heated through.

BROCCOLI CREAM SOUP
Makes 4 to 6 servings

1 tablespoon olive oil

2 cups chopped onions

1 pound fresh broccoli florets
   or spears

2 cups vegetable broth

6 tablespoons cream cheese

1 cup milk

¾ teaspoon salt

⅛ teaspoon ground red pepper

⅓ cup finely chopped green
   onions

1 Heat oil in large saucepan over medium-high heat. Add onions; cook and stir 4 minutes or until translucent. Add broccoli and broth; bring to a boil. Reduce heat to medium-low; cover and simmer 10 minutes or until broccoli is tender.

2 Working in batches, purée soup in food processor or blender (or use immersion blender). Return soup to saucepan; heat over medium heat.

3 Whisk in cream cheese until melted. Stir in milk, salt and red pepper; cook 2 minutes or until heated through. Top with green onions.

SPINACH NOODLE BOWL *with* GINGER

Makes 4 servings

6 cups chicken broth

4 ounces uncooked vermicelli noodles, broken into thirds

1½ cups matchstick carrots

3 ounces snow peas, stemmed and halved

4 cups packed spinach leaves (4 ounces)

1½ cups cooked shrimp or cubed chicken *or* 1 package (14 ounces) firm tofu, drained and cubed

½ cup finely chopped green onions

1 tablespoon grated fresh ginger

1 teaspoon soy sauce

⅛ to ¼ teaspoon red pepper flakes

1 Bring broth to a boil in Dutch oven over high heat. Add vermicelli; return to a boil. Cook 2 minutes less than package directions for al dente. Add carrots and snow peas; cook 2 minutes or until noodles are tender.

2 Remove from heat; stir in spinach, shrimp, green onions, ginger, soy sauce and red pepper flakes. Let stand 2 minutes before serving.

SANDWICHES & WRAPS

CHERRY and CHEESE PANINI
Makes 4 servings

1 tablespoon olive oil

1 large red onion, thinly sliced

¼ teaspoon dried thyme

2 teaspoons balsamic vinegar

⅛ teaspoon salt

⅛ teaspoon black pepper

½ cup fresh sweet cherries, pitted and chopped

4 ounces blue cheese, at room temperature

3 ounces cream cheese, softened

8 large thin slices Italian or country-style bread

1 to 2 tablespoons butter

1 Heat oil in large skillet over medium heat. Add onion and thyme; cook and stir 3 minutes or until onion is tender. Add vinegar, salt and pepper, stirring to scrape up any browned bits from bottom of skillet. Transfer onion mixture to medium bowl; stir in cherries.

2 Mash blue cheese and cream cheese in small bowl until blended. Spread evenly over four bread slices. Top each slice with one fourth of cherry mixture (about ⅓ cup) and remaining bread slices.

3 Wipe out skillet. Melt 1 tablespoon butter in skillet. Add two sandwiches; press down with spatula. Cook over medium heat 3 to 4 minutes per side or until golden. Repeat with remaining sandwiches, adding more butter if necessary.

CHICKEN *and* GRAPE PITA SANDWICHES

Makes 6 servings

4 **cups water**

1 **teaspoon salt**

1 **pound boneless skinless chicken breasts, cut into ½-inch pieces**

½ **cup plain yogurt**

¼ **cup mayonnaise**

2 **tablespoons fresh tarragon leaves, minced *or* 2 teaspoons dried tarragon**

2 **teaspoons Dijon mustard**

2 **teaspoons honey**

½ **teaspoon black pepper**

1 **cup thinly sliced celery**

1 **cup red seedless grapes, cut into halves**

1 **medium head red leaf lettuce**

3 **pita bread rounds, cut in half crosswise**

1 Bring water and salt to a boil in large saucepan. Add chicken; cover and remove from heat. Let stand 6 minutes or until chicken is cooked through (165°F). Drain and rinse chicken under cold water to cool.

2 Stir yogurt, mayonnaise, tarragon, mustard, honey and pepper in large bowl until well blended. Add chicken, celery and grapes; stir to coat evenly.

3 Separate lettuce leaves. Select six large leaves and discard stems. Tear or shred remaining leaves.

4 Line each pita half with whole lettuce leaf. Fill with torn lettuce leaves and about ⅔ cup chicken mixture.

NIÇOISE SALAD WRAPS
Makes 2 servings

½ **cup green bean pieces (½-inch pieces)**

2 **medium red potatoes, each cut into 8 wedges**

2 **tablespoons vinaigrette, divided**

1 **egg**

2 **cups watercress leaves**

1 **can (5 ounces) water-packed albacore tuna, drained and flaked**

8 **niçoise olives, pitted and halved**

3 **cherry tomatoes, quartered**

Salt and black pepper

2 **(10-inch) whole wheat tortillas**

1 Bring 8 cups water to a boil in large saucepan. Add green beans and potatoes. Reduce heat to low; simmer 6 minutes or until tender. Remove vegetables with slotted spoon; plunge in ice water to stop cooking. Drain on paper towels. Transfer to medium bowl; toss with 1 tablespoon vinaigrette.

2 Return water to a boil. Add whole egg; reduce heat and simmer 12 minutes. Run under cool water to stop cooking. Peel and cut into eight wedges.

3 Add watercress, tuna, olives, tomatoes and remaining 1 tablespoon vinaigrette to vegetables; toss gently. Season with salt and pepper.

4 Heat tortillas in nonstick skillet over medium-high heat until softened, turning once. Place on plates.

5 Divide salad between tortillas; top with egg wedges. Roll up tortillas to enclose filling.

MUSHROOM TOFU BURGERS

Makes 6 servings

- **7 ounces extra firm tofu**
- **3 teaspoons olive oil, divided**
- **8 ounces cremini mushrooms, coarsely chopped**
- **½ medium onion, coarsely chopped**
- **1 clove garlic, minced**
- **1 cup old-fashioned oats**
- **⅓ cup finely chopped walnuts**
- **1 egg**
- **½ teaspoon salt**
- **½ teaspoon onion powder**
- **¼ teaspoon dried thyme**
- **6 multi-grain English muffins, split and toasted**
- **Lettuce, tomato and red onion slices (optional)**

1. Crumble tofu and spread on small baking sheet or freezer-safe plate. Freeze 1 hour or until firm.

2. Heat 1 teaspoon oil in large nonstick skillet over medium heat. Add mushrooms, onion and garlic; cook and stir 10 minutes or until mushrooms are tender and any water from mushrooms has evaporated. Remove from heat; cool slightly.

3. Combine mushroom mixture, tofu, oats, walnuts, egg, salt, onion powder and thyme in food processor or blender; process until combined. (Some tofu pieces may remain). Shape mixture into six ⅓-cup patties.

4. Heat 1 teaspoon oil in same skillet over medium-low heat. Working in batches, cook patties 5 minutes per side, adding additional oil as needed.

5. Serve burgers on English muffins with lettuce, tomato and red onion, if desired.

SPICY EGGPLANT BURGERS

Makes 4 servings

1 **eggplant (about 1 pound), peeled**

  Salt and black pepper

2 **egg whites**

½ **cup Italian-style panko bread crumbs**

4 **slices pepper jack cheese**

4 **whole wheat hamburger buns**

¼ **cup chipotle mayonnaise or regular mayonnaise**

  Baby spinach leaves and thinly sliced tomato

1 Preheat oven to 375°F. Spray baking sheet with nonstick cooking spray.

2 Cut four ½-inch-thick slices from widest part of eggplant. Season both sides of eggplant with salt and pepper. Whisk egg whites in shallow bowl. Place panko in another shallow bowl.

3 Dip eggplant slices in egg whites; dredge in panko, pressing gently to adhere. Place on prepared baking sheet.

4 Bake 30 minutes or until eggplant is tender and panko is golden brown, turning once halfway through baking. Place one slice of cheese on each eggplant slice; bake 1 minute or until softened.

5 Serve eggplant on buns with mayonnaise, spinach and tomato.

TIP: To make chipotle mayonnaise, stir ½ teaspoon minced chipotle peppers in adobo sauce into ¼ cup mayonnaise in small bowl. Or use chipotle chili powder to taste.

BELL PEPPER *and* BLACK BEAN BURRITOS

Makes 6 servings

2 teaspoons canola oil

1½ cups diced red, yellow and green bell peppers *or* 1 large green bell pepper, diced

½ cup chopped onion

1 can (about 15 ounces) black beans, rinsed and drained

½ cup salsa

1 teaspoon chili powder

6 (8-inch) whole wheat flour tortillas, warmed

¾ cup (3 ounces) shredded Cheddar cheese or Mexican cheese blend

½ cup chopped fresh cilantro

1 Heat oil in large skillet over medium heat. Add bell peppers and onion; cook and stir 5 minutes or until softened. Stir in beans, salsa and chili powder; cook and stir 5 to 8 minutes or until vegetables are tender and sauce is thickened.

2 Spoon about ⅔ cup bean mixture down center of each tortilla. Top with cheese and cilantro. Roll up to enclose filling.

CAPRESE PORTOBELLO BURGERS

Makes 4 servings

3 **ounces mozzarella cheese, diced**

2 **plum tomatoes, chopped**

2 **tablespoons chopped fresh basil**

1 **tablespoon balsamic vinaigrette**

1 **clove garlic, crushed**

¼ **teaspoon salt**

⅛ **teaspoon black pepper**

4 **portobello mushrooms (about 12 ounces), gills and stems removed**

4 **whole wheat sandwich thin rounds or sandwich rolls**

1 Prepare grill for direct cooking. Oil grid.

2 Combine cheese, tomatoes, basil, vinaigrette, garlic, salt and pepper in small bowl.

3 Grill mushrooms over medium-high heat 5 minutes per side. Turn cap sides down and fill with tomato mixture; grill, covered, 3 minutes or until cheese is melted.

4 Place sandwich thins on grid; grill until toasted. Serve mushrooms on sandwich thins.

ENTRÉES

STEAK PARMESAN
Makes 2 to 4 servings

4 cloves garlic, minced

1 tablespoon olive oil

1 tablespoon coarse salt

1 teaspoon dried rosemary

1 teaspoon black pepper

2 beef T-bone or Porterhouse steaks, cut 1 inch thick (about 2 pounds)

¼ cup grated Parmesan cheese

1 Prepare grill for direct cooking.

2 Combine garlic, oil, salt, rosemary and pepper in small bowl; press into both sides of steaks. Let stand 15 minutes.

3 Grill steaks, covered, over medium-high heat 7 to 9 minutes per side for medium rare (145°F) or to desired doneness.

4 Transfer steaks to cutting board; sprinkle with cheese. Tent with foil; let stand 5 minutes before serving.

TIP: For a smoky flavor, soak 2 cups hickory or oak wood chips in cold water to cover at least 30 minutes. Drain and scatter over hot coals before grilling. If you're using a gas grill, place the soaked wood chips in a cast iron smoker box and place the box on the grid with the steaks.

BUTTERNUT SQUASH GNOCCHI *with* SAVORY HERB BUTTER

Makes 4 servings

1 butternut squash (about 2½ pounds), peeled, seeded and cut into 1-inch pieces

1 cup all-purpose flour, plus additional for work surface

3½ teaspoons salt, divided

¼ teaspoon black pepper

4 quarts water

¼ cup (½ stick) butter

2 teaspoons minced garlic

1 teaspoon dried parsley flakes

1 teaspoon rubbed sage

½ teaspoon dried thyme

Juice of 1 lemon

¼ cup shredded Parmesan cheese

1 Place squash in large microwavable bowl; cover with vented plastic wrap. Microwave on HIGH 6 to 7 minutes or until very tender. Let stand 10 minutes to cool slightly. Drain.

2 Mash squash or press through ricer into medium bowl. Add 1 cup flour, 2 teaspoons salt and pepper; mix well.

3 Dust cutting board or work surface with flour. Working in batches, scoop portions of dough onto board and roll into ½-inch-thick rope using floured hands. Cut each rope into ¾-inch pieces.

4 Bring water and 1 teaspoon salt to a boil in large saucepan over high heat. Working in batches, drop 8 to 12 gnocchi into boiling water; cook about 2½ minutes or until gnocchi float to surface. Remove gnocchi with slotted spoon; drain on paper towels. Return water to a boil between batches.

5 Melt butter in large nonstick skillet over medium heat. Add garlic, parsley flakes, sage, thyme and remaining ½ teaspoon salt; cook just until butter begins to brown, stirring occasionally. Add lemon juice; cook 30 seconds. Add gnocchi; gently stir to coat. Cook 2 minutes or until lightly browned and heated through. Serve with cheese.

ORECCHIETTE *with* SAUSAGE *and* BROCCOLI RABE

Makes 4 to 6 servings

- **1 tablespoon olive oil**
- **1 pound mild Italian sausage, casings removed**
- **2 cloves garlic, minced**
- **⅛ teaspoon red pepper flakes**
- **1½ pounds broccoli rabe, stems trimmed, cut into 2-inch pieces**
- **1 package (16 ounces) uncooked orecchiette pasta**
- **¾ cup grated Parmesan cheese**
- **Salt and black pepper**

1 Bring large pot of salted water to a boil.

2 Meanwhile, heat oil in large skillet over medium-high heat. Add sausage; cook about 8 minutes or until browned, stirring to break up meat into bite-size pieces. Drain fat. Add garlic and red pepper flakes; cook and stir 3 minutes.

3 Add broccoli rabe to boiling water; cook 2 minutes. Remove with slotted spoon; transfer to skillet with sausage mixture. Cook over medium-low heat until crisp-tender, stirring occasionally.

4 Add pasta to boiling water; cook according to package directions for al dente. Drain pasta, reserving 1 cup cooking water. Combine pasta, sausage mixture and Parmesan in large serving bowl; mix well. Stir in enough reserved cooking water until mixture is saucy and pasta is coated. Season with salt and pepper to taste. Serve immediately.

BREADED VEAL SCALLOPINI *with* MIXED MUSHROOMS

Makes 2 servings

- **8 ounces veal cutlets or thin pork chops**
- **½ teaspoon salt, divided**
- **¼ teaspoon black pepper, divided**
- **1 egg**
- **1 tablespoon milk or water**
- **½ cup plain dry bread crumbs**
- **5 tablespoons butter, divided**
- **2 tablespoons olive oil, divided**
- **2 large shallots, chopped**
- **8 ounces assorted fresh mushrooms, such as cremini, oyster and shiitake**
- **½ teaspoon herbes de Provence**
- **½ cup chicken broth**
- **Lemon wedges (optional)**

1 Season cutlets with ¼ teaspoon salt and ⅛ teaspoon pepper. Whisk egg and milk in shallow bowl. Place bread crumbs in another shallow bow.

2 Dip cutlets into egg mixture, letting excess drip back into bowl. Coat with bread crumbs.

3 Heat 1 tablespoon butter and 1 tablespoon oil in large nonstick skillet over medium-high heat. Cook half of cutlets 3 minutes or until golden brown and cooked through, turning once. Transfer to plate. Add 1 tablespoon butter and remaining 1 tablespoon oil; repeat with remaining cutlets.

4 Wipe out skillet with paper towel. Melt remaining 3 tablespoons butter over medium-high heat. Add shallots; cook and stir 1 to 2 minutes or until translucent. Add mushrooms, remaining ¼ teaspoon salt, ⅛ teaspoon pepper and herbes de Provence; cook and stir 3 to 4 minutes or until most of liquid is evaporated. Stir in broth; cook 2 to 3 minutes or until slightly thickened.

5 Pour mushroom mixture over cutlets. Garnish with lemon wedges.

LINGUINE *with* HERBS, TOMATOES *and* CAPERS

Makes 4 servings

12 ounces uncooked linguine

2 tablespoons olive oil

2 cloves garlic, minced

2 cups chopped fresh tomatoes

¼ cup finely chopped green onions

3 tablespoons drained capers

2 tablespoons finely chopped fresh basil

¼ teaspoon salt

⅛ teaspoon black pepper

½ cup shredded Parmesan cheese

1 Cook linguine in large saucepan of salted boiling water according to package directions for al dente. Drain and return to saucepan; keep warm.

2 Meanwhile, heat oil in large skillet over medium-high heat. Add garlic and tomatoes; cook 3 minutes or until tomatoes begin to soften, stirring frequently. Stir in green onions, capers and basil. Season with salt and pepper.

3 Add linguine to skillet; toss with tomato mixture. Sprinkle with cheese just before serving.

LEMON-DIJON CHICKEN *with* POTATOES

Makes 6 servings

2 medium lemons, halved

½ cup chopped fresh parsley

2 tablespoons Dijon mustard

4 cloves garlic, minced

2 teaspoons olive oil

1 teaspoon dried rosemary

¾ teaspoon black pepper

½ teaspoon salt

1 whole chicken (about 4 pounds)

1½ pounds small red potatoes, halved

1 Preheat oven to 350°F.

2 Squeeze 3 tablespoons juice from lemons; reserve squeezed lemon halves. Combine lemon juice, parsley, mustard, garlic, oil, rosemary, pepper and salt in small bowl; mix well. Reserve 2 tablespoons mixture.

3 Place chicken on rack in shallow roasting pan. Gently slide fingers between skin and meat of chicken breasts and drumsticks to separate skin from meat, being careful not to tear skin. Spoon parsley mixture between skin and meat. (Secure breast skin with toothpicks, if necessary.) Discard any remaining parsley mixture. Place lemon halves in cavity of chicken. Bake 30 minutes.

4 Meanwhile, toss potatoes with reserved parsley mixture in medium bowl until coated. Arrange potatoes around chicken; bake 1 hour or until juices in chicken run clear and thermometer inserted into thickest part of thigh registers 165°F. Remove chicken from oven; let stand 10 minutes. Remove skin; slice chicken. Serve with potatoes.

BUTTERNUT SQUASH MAC *and* CHEESE

Makes 6 to 8 servings

1 small butternut squash, peeled, seeded and cubed

1 tablespoon olive oil

1¼ teaspoons salt, divided

1 package (16 ounces) uncooked large elbow macaroni or cavatappi pasta

½ cup (1 stick) butter, divided

¼ cup all-purpose flour

1½ cups milk

¼ teaspoon ground nutmeg

⅛ teaspoon ground red pepper

2 cups (8 ounces) shredded Cheddar cheese

1 cup (4 ounces) shredded Monterey Jack cheese

1 cup panko bread crumbs

½ cup chopped hazelnuts or walnuts

⅛ teaspoon dried sage

1 cup (4 ounces) shredded Chihuahua cheese*

*If Chihuahua cheese is not available, substitute additional Monterey Jack cheese.

1 Preheat oven to 350°F. Spread squash on large rimmed baking sheet; drizzle with oil and sprinkle with ¼ teaspoon salt. Bake 20 minutes or until squash is very tender, stirring once.

2 Spray 2-quart baking dish with nonstick cooking spray. Cook macaroni in large saucepan of boiling salted water according to package directions for al dente. Drain.

3 Meanwhile, melt ¼ cup butter in medium saucepan over medium-high heat. Whisk in flour until smooth; cook 1 minute without browning, whisking constantly. Gradually whisk in milk in thin steady stream. Add ¾ teaspoon salt, nutmeg and red pepper; cook 2 to 3 minutes or until thickened, stirring frequently. Gradually add Cheddar and Monterey Jack cheeses, stirring after each addition until smooth. Stir in squash; cook 1 minute or until heated through, stirring constantly. Pour sauce over pasta; stir to coat.

4 Meanwhile, melt remaining ¼ cup butter in small skillet over medium-low heat; cook until golden brown. Remove from heat; stir in panko, hazelnuts, sage and remaining ¼ teaspoon salt.

5 Layer half of pasta in prepared baking dish; sprinkle with ½ cup Chihuahua cheese. Top with remaining pasta. Sprinkle with remaining Chihuahua cheese; top with panko mixture.

6 Bake 25 to 30 minutes or until topping is golden brown and pasta is heated through.

PUMPKIN CURRY

Makes 4 servings

1 tablespoon vegetable oil

1 package (14 ounces) extra firm tofu, drained and cut into 1-inch cubes

¼ cup Thai red curry paste

2 cloves garlic, minced

1 can (14 ounces) coconut milk

1 can (15 ounces) pumpkin purée

1 cup water

1½ teaspoons salt

1 teaspoon sriracha sauce

4 cups cut-up vegetables (broccoli, cauliflower, red bell pepper, sweet potato)

½ cup peas

3 cups hot cooked rice

¼ cup shredded fresh basil

1 Heat oil in wok or large skillet over high heat. Add tofu; cook 2 to 3 minutes or until lightly browned, turning occasionally. Add curry paste and garlic; cook 1 minute or until tofu is coated. Add coconut milk, pumpkin, water, salt and sriracha; bring to a boil. Stir in vegetables.

2 Reduce heat to medium; cover and simmer 20 minutes or until vegetables are tender. Stir in peas; cook 1 minute or until heated through. Serve over rice; top with basil.

POT ROAST *with* BACON *and* MUSHROOMS

Makes 6 to 8 servings

6 slices bacon, chopped

1 boneless beef chuck roast (2½ to 3 pounds), trimmed*

¾ teaspoon salt, divided

¼ teaspoon black pepper

¾ cup chopped shallots

8 ounces sliced white mushrooms

¼ ounce dried porcini mushrooms (optional)

4 cloves garlic, minced

1 teaspoon dried oregano

1 cup chicken broth

2 tablespoons tomato paste

Roasted Cauliflower (recipe follows, optional)

If your slow cooker is less than 5 quarts, cut any roast larger than 2½ pounds in half so it cooks completely.

SLOW COOKER DIRECTIONS

1 Cook bacon in large skillet over medium heat until crisp, stirring frequently. Remove to paper towel-lined plate using slotted spoon.

2 Drain all but 2 tablespoons drippings from skillet. Season roast with ½ teaspoon salt and pepper. Heat same skillet over medium-high heat. Add roast; cook 8 minutes or until well browned. Transfer roast to large plate.

3 Add shallots, white mushrooms, porcini mushrooms, if desired, garlic, oregano and remaining ¼ teaspoon salt to same skillet; cook 3 to 4 minutes or until softened. Transfer to slow cooker; stir in bacon. Top with roast.

4 Whisk broth and tomato paste in small bowl until well blended. Pour broth mixture over roast. Cover; cook on LOW 8 hours.

5 Prepare Roasted Cauliflower, if desired. Transfer roast to large cutting board. Let stand 10 minutes before slicing. Top each serving with mushroom sauce from slow cooker and serve with Roasted Cauliflower.

ROASTED CAULIFLOWER: Preheat oven to 375°F. Break 1 head cauliflower into florets; spread on large baking sheet. Drizzle with olive oil and season with salt and pepper; toss to coat. Roast 20 minutes. Stir; roast 15 minutes or until tender.

WINTER SQUASH RISOTTO

Makes 4 to 6 servings

4 to 5 cups vegetable broth

2 tablespoons olive oil

1 small butternut squash or medium delicata squash, peeled and cut into 1-inch pieces (about 2 cups)

1 large shallot or small onion, finely chopped

½ teaspoon paprika

¼ teaspoon dried thyme

¼ teaspoon salt

¼ teaspoon black pepper

1 cup uncooked arborio rice

¼ cup dry white wine

1 cup grated Parmesan or Romano cheese, divided

1 Bring broth to a simmer in medium saucepan.

2 Heat oil in large nonstick skillet over medium heat. Add squash; cook and stir 3 minutes. Add shallot; cook and stir 3 to 4 minutes or until squash is almost tender. Stir in paprika, thyme, salt and pepper. Add rice; stir to coat.

3 Add wine; cook and stir until wine is absorbed. Add broth, ½ cup at a time, stirring frequently until broth is absorbed before adding next ½ cup. Continue adding broth and stirring until rice is tender and mixture is creamy, about 20 to 25 minutes. Stir in ¾ cup cheese.

4 Scoop risotto into bowls; sprinkle with remaining ¼ cup cheese.

PECAN CATFISH *with* CRANBERRY COMPOTE

Makes 4 servings

CRANBERRY COMPOTE

- 1 **package (12 ounces) fresh cranberries**
- ¾ **cup water**
- ½ **cup granulated sugar**
- ¼ **cup orange juice**
- 2 **tablespoons packed dark brown sugar**
- 2 **teaspoons grated fresh ginger**
- ¼ **teaspoon Chinese five-spice powder**
- ⅛ **teaspoon salt**
- 1 **teaspoon butter**

FISH

- 1½ **cups pecans**
- 2 **tablespoons all-purpose flour**
- 1 **egg**
- 2 **tablespoons water**
  Salt and black pepper
- 4 **catfish fillets (about 1¼ pounds)**
- 2 **tablespoons butter, divided**

1 For compote, combine cranberries, ¾ cup water, granulated sugar, orange juice, brown sugar, ginger, five-spice powder and ⅛ teaspoon salt in large saucepan. Cook over medium-high heat 10 minutes or until berries begin to pop, stirring occasionally.

2 Cook and stir 5 minutes or until cranberries are saucy. Remove from heat; stir in 1 teaspoon butter. Let cool; refrigerate at least 3 hours. Compote can be made up to 1 week in advance; store in refrigerator.

3 For fish, preheat oven to 425°F. Place pecans and flour in food processor; pulse just until finely chopped. Transfer to shallow dish. Whisk egg and 2 tablespoons water in another shallow dish. Season both sides of each fillet with salt and pepper; dip in egg, letting excess drip back into bowl. Coat with pecan mixture.

4 Melt 1 tablespoon butter; evenly brush over bottom of 13×9-inch baking pan.

5 Place fillets in single layer in prepared pan. Dot with remaining 1 tablespoon butter. Bake 15 to 20 minutes or until fish just begins to flake when tested with fork. Serve with compote.

HONEY LEMON GARLIC CHICKEN

Makes 4 servings

2 **lemons, divided**

2 **tablespoons butter, melted**

2 **tablespoons honey**

3 **cloves garlic, chopped**

2 **sprigs fresh rosemary, leaves removed from stems**

1 **teaspoon salt**

½ **teaspoon black pepper**

3 **pounds chicken (4 bone-in skin-on chicken thighs and 4 drumsticks)**

1¼ **pounds potatoes, cut into halves or quarters**

1 Preheat oven to 375°F. Grate peel and squeeze juice from one lemon. Cut remaining lemon into slices.

2 Combine lemon peel, lemon juice, butter, honey, garlic, rosemary leaves, salt and pepper in small bowl; mix well. Combine chicken, potatoes and lemon slices in large bowl. Pour butter mixture over chicken and potatoes; toss to coat. Arrange in single layer on large rimmed baking sheet or in shallow roasting pan.

3 Bake about 1 hour or until potatoes are tender and chicken is cooked through (165°F). Cover loosely with foil if chicken skin is browning too quickly.

VEGETABLES & SIDES

ROASTED ASPARAGUS *with* ORANGE BUTTER

Makes 4 servings

1 pound asparagus, trimmed

2 tablespoons butter, melted

2 tablespoons orange juice

½ teaspoon salt

¼ teaspoon black pepper

1½ teaspoons finely shredded or grated orange peel

1 Preheat oven to 425°F.

2 Place asparagus in shallow 1½-quart baking dish. Combine butter and orange juice in small bowl; drizzle over asparagus. Sprinkle with salt and pepper; turn to coat.

3 Roast 12 minutes for medium-sized asparagus or until asparagus is crisp-tender. Top with orange peel.

CRISPY OVEN FRIES *with* HERBED MAYONNAISE

Makes 2 servings

Herbed Mayonnaise (recipe follows)

2 large unpeeled russet potatoes

2 tablespoons vegetable oil

1 teaspoon kosher salt

1 Preheat oven to 425°F. Line two baking sheets with foil; spray with nonstick cooking spray. Prepare Herbed Mayonnaise.

2 Cut potatoes lengthwise into ¼-inch slices, then cut each slice into ¼-inch strips. Combine potato strips and oil on prepared baking sheets. Toss to coat evenly; arrange in single layer.

3 Bake 25 minutes. Turn fries over; bake 15 minutes or until light golden brown and crisp. Sprinkle with salt. Serve immediately with Herbed Mayonnaise.

HERBED MAYONNAISE: Stir ½ cup mayonnaise, 2 tablespoons chopped fresh herbs (such as basil, parsley, oregano and/or dill), 1 teaspoon salt and ½ teaspoon black pepper in small bowl until smooth and well blended. Cover and refrigerate until ready to serve.

CORN PUDDING

Makes 8 servings

1 tablespoon butter

1 small onion, chopped

1 tablespoon all-purpose flour

2 cups half-and-half

1 cup milk

¼ cup quick-cooking grits or polenta

2 cups corn

4 eggs, lightly beaten

1 can (4 ounces) diced mild green chiles, drained

¾ teaspoon salt

¼ teaspoon black pepper

¼ teaspoon hot pepper sauce

1 Preheat oven to 325°F. Grease 11×7-inch baking dish.

2 Melt butter in large saucepan over medium heat. Add onion; cook and stir about 7 minutes or until tender and lightly browned. Stir in flour; cook until golden, stirring frequently. Whisk in half-and-half and milk. Bring to a boil.

3 Whisk in grits; reduce heat to medium-low. Cook and stir 10 minutes or until mixture is thickened. Remove from heat. Stir in corn, eggs, chiles, salt, black pepper and hot pepper sauce. Pour into prepared baking dish.

4 Bake 1 hour or until knife inserted into center comes out clean.

MARINATED CUCUMBERS

Makes 4 to 6 servings

1 large cucumber

2 tablespoons unseasoned rice vinegar

2 tablespoons peanut or vegetable oil

2 tablespoons soy sauce

1½ teaspoons sugar

1 clove garlic, minced

¼ teaspoon red pepper flakes

1 Score cucumber lengthwise with tines of fork. Cut in half lengthwise; scrape out and discard seeds. Cut crosswise into ⅛-inch slices; place in medium bowl.

2 Whisk vinegar, oil, soy sauce, sugar, garlic and red pepper flakes in small bowl; pour over cucumber and toss to coat. Cover; refrigerate at least 4 hours or up to 2 days.

MEDITERRANEAN ROASTED VEGETABLES

Makes 6 servings

1½ **pounds red or yellow potatoes, cut into ½-inch wedges**

4 **whole tomatoes (optional)**

1 **tablespoon plus 1½ teaspoons olive oil, divided**

1 **red bell pepper, cut into ½-inch pieces**

1 **yellow or orange bell pepper, cut into ½-inch pieces**

1 **small red onion, cut into ½-inch wedges**

2 **cloves garlic, minced**

½ **teaspoon salt**

¼ **teaspoon black pepper**

1 **tablespoon balsamic vinegar**

¼ **cup chopped fresh basil**

1 Preheat oven to 425°F. Spray large roasting pan with nonstick cooking spray.

2 Place potatoes and tomatoes, if desired, in prepared pan. Drizzle with 1 tablespoon oil; toss to coat evenly. Roast 10 minutes.

3 Add bell peppers and onion to pan. Drizzle with remaining 1½ teaspoons oil. Sprinkle with garlic, salt and black pepper; toss to coat evenly.

4 Roast 18 to 20 minutes or until vegetables are browned and tender, stirring once.

5 Transfer vegetables to large serving dish. Drizzle vinegar over vegetables; toss to coat evenly. Add basil; toss again. Serve warm or at room temperature.

GREEN BEAN *and* EGG SALAD
Makes 6 servings

1 **pound green beans, trimmed and cut into 2-inch pieces**

3 **hard-cooked eggs, peeled and chopped**

2 **stalks celery, cut into slices**

½ **cup Cheddar cheese cubes (¼-inch cubes)**

¼ **cup chopped red onion**

⅓ **cup mayonnaise**

2 **teaspoons cider vinegar**

1½ **teaspoons sugar**

½ **teaspoon salt**

½ **teaspoon celery seed**

⅛ **teaspoon black pepper**

1 Bring large saucepan of salted water to a boil. Add green beans; cook 4 minutes or until crisp-tender. Drain and rinse under cold running water to stop cooking.

2 Combine beans, eggs, celery, cheese and onion in large bowl. Combine mayonnaise, vinegar, sugar, salt, celery seed and pepper in small bowl; mix well. Add to bean mixture; mix gently until coated.

3 Cover and refrigerate at least 1 hour before serving.

CREAMED KALE
Makes 8 servings

- **2 large bunches kale (about 2 pounds)**
- **2 tablespoons butter**
- **2 tablespoons all-purpose flour**
- **1½ cups milk**
- **½ cup shredded Parmesan cheese, plus additional for garnish**
- **2 cloves garlic, minced**
- **¼ teaspoon salt**
- **⅛ teaspoon ground nutmeg**

1 Remove stems from kale; discard. Coarsely chop leaves. Bring large saucepan of water to a boil. Add kale; cook 5 minutes. Drain.

2 Melt butter in large saucepan over medium heat. Whisk in flour; cook 1 minute without browning. Gradually whisk in milk until well blended. Cook 4 to 5 minutes or until sauce boils and is thickened, whisking constantly. Whisk in ½ cup cheese, garlic, salt and nutmeg.

3 Remove saucepan from heat. Stir in kale until combined. Sprinkle with additional cheese, if desired.

SNACKS

BEANS *and* GREENS CROSTINI
Makes about 24 crostini

4 tablespoons olive oil, divided

1 small onion, thinly sliced

4 cups thinly sliced Italian black kale or other dinosaur kale variety

2 tablespoons minced garlic, divided

1 tablespoon balsamic vinegar

2 teaspoons salt, divided

¼ teaspoon red pepper flakes

1 can (about 15 ounces) cannellini beans, rinsed and drained

1 tablespoon chopped fresh rosemary

Toasted baguette slices

1 Heat 1 tablespoon oil in large nonstick skillet over medium heat. Add onion; cook and stir 5 minutes or until softened. Add kale and 1 tablespoon garlic; cook and stir 15 minutes or until kale is softened and most of liquid has evaporated. Stir in vinegar, 1 teaspoon salt and red pepper flakes.

2 Combine beans, remaining 3 tablespoons oil, 1 tablespoon garlic, 1 teaspoon salt and rosemary in food processor; process until smooth.

3 Spread bean mixture over baguette slices; top with kale.

STUFFED VEGETABLE TEMPURA
Makes 4 servings

½ cup all-purpose flour

2 tablespoons plus ½ teaspoon cornstarch, divided

1 teaspoon baking powder

¼ teaspoon salt

¾ cup cold water

1 egg, separated

1 pound large raw shrimp, peeled and deveined

1 tablespoon soy sauce

2 teaspoons toasted sesame oil

Soy Dipping Sauce (page 111)

4 cups vegetable oil

1 zucchini, diagonally cut into ½-inch-thick slices

8 white or cremini mushrooms, stems removed

1 red bell pepper, cut into wedges

1 green bell pepper, cut into wedges

1 For batter, whisk flour, 2 tablespoons cornstarch, baking powder and salt in medium bowl. Make well in center and whisk in cold water until batter is consistency of pancake batter with small lumps. Add egg white; whisk until blended. Cover and refrigerate 30 minutes.

2 Meanwhile, place egg yolk in food processor. Add shrimp, soy sauce, sesame oil and remaining ½ teaspoon cornstarch. Process until shrimp is chopped to a paste. Place shrimp paste in small bowl; cover and refrigerate.

3 Prepare Soy Dipping Sauce; keep warm.

4 Heat vegetable oil in wok over medium-high heat until oil registers 375°F on deep-fry thermometer; adjust heat to maintain temperature during cooking. Spread about 2 teaspoons shrimp paste on 8 zucchini slices and stuff remaining paste into mushroom caps and pepper wedges.

5 Stir batter and dip stuffed vegetables into batter. Carefully add to hot oil in batches, stuffing sides up. Fry about 2 minutes for peppers, 3 minutes for zucchini and 4 minutes for mushrooms or until golden brown, turning once. Drain on paper towels. Dip unstuffed zucchini slices into remaining batter and fry about 3 minutes or until golden brown.

6 Serve with Soy Dipping Sauce.

SOY DIPPING SAUCE
Makes about 1¼ cups

1 cup vegetable broth

3 tablespoons soy sauce

2 tablespoons sugar

1 tablespoon sake or rice wine

¼ teaspoon ground ginger

1 Combine vegetable broth, soy sauce, sugar, sake and ground ginger in small saucepan. Bring to a boil over medium heat.

2 Remove from heat; keep warm until ready to serve.

111

KALE CHIPS

Makes 6 servings

1 **large bunch kale (about 1 pound)**

1 **to 2 tablespoons olive oil**

1 **teaspoon garlic salt, seasoned salt or regular salt**

1 Preheat oven to 350°F. Line baking sheets with parchment paper.

2 Wash kale and pat dry with paper towels. Remove center ribs and stems; discard. Cut leaves into 2- to 3-inch-wide pieces.

3 Combine leaves, oil and garlic salt in large bowl; toss to coat. Spread onto prepared baking sheets.

4 Bake 10 to 15 minutes or until edges are lightly browned and leaves are crisp.* Cool completely on baking sheets. Store in airtight container.

*If the leaves are lightly browned but not crisp, turn oven off and let chips stand in oven until crisp, about 10 minutes. Do not keep the oven on as the chips will burn easily.

CORN FRITTERS

Makes 8 fritters

2 **large ears corn**

2 **eggs, separated**

¼ **cup all-purpose flour**

1 **tablespoon sugar**

1 **tablespoon butter, melted**

¼ **teaspoon salt**

⅛ **teaspoon black pepper**

⅛ **teaspoon cream of tartar**

1 **to 2 tablespoons vegetable oil**

1 Husk corn. Cut kernels from ears; place in medium bowl. Hold cobs over bowl, scraping with back of knife to extract juice. Transfer about half of kernels to food processor; process 2 to 3 seconds or until coarsely chopped. Add to whole kernels.

2 Whisk egg yolks in large bowl. Whisk in flour, sugar, butter, salt and pepper. Stir in corn mixture.

3 Beat egg whites and cream of tartar in separate large bowl with electric mixer at high speed until stiff peaks form. Fold egg whites into corn mixture.

4 Heat 1 tablespoon oil in 12-inch nonstick skillet over medium-high heat. Drop ¼ cupfuls of batter into skillet 1-inch apart. Cook 3 to 5 minutes per side or until lightly browned. Repeat with remaining batter, adding additional oil as needed. Serve hot.

GOAT CHEESE CROSTINI *with* SWEET ONION JAM

Makes 24 crostini

1 tablespoon olive oil

2 medium yellow onions, thinly sliced

¾ cup dry red wine

¼ cup water

2 tablespoons packed brown sugar

1 tablespoon balsamic vinegar

1 teaspoon salt

¼ teaspoon black pepper

4 ounces soft goat cheese

4 ounces cream cheese, softened

2 teaspoons chopped fresh thyme, plus additional for garnish

1 loaf (16 ounces) French bread, cut into 24 slices (about 1 inch thick), lightly toasted

1 Heat oil in large skillet over medium heat. Add onions; cook and stir 10 minutes. Add wine, water, brown sugar, vinegar, salt and pepper; bring to a simmer. Reduce heat to low; cook, uncovered, 15 to 20 minutes or until all liquid is absorbed. (If mixture appears dry, stir in a few additional tablespoons of water.) Cool 30 minutes or cover and refrigerate until ready to use.

2 Meanwhile, stir goat cheese, cream cheese and 2 teaspoons thyme in small bowl until well blended.

3 Spread goat cheese mixture on bread slices; top with onion jam. Garnish with additional thyme.

TOMATOES STUFFED *with* GARLIC POTATO SALAD

Makes 6 servings

1 **pound russet potatoes, peeled and cut into ¼-inch cubes**

3 **tablespoons red or white wine vinegar, divided**

½ **cup mayonnaise**

2 **tablespoons minced fresh parsley, plus additional for garnish**

2 **cloves garlic, minced**

1 **teaspoon salt**

⅛ **teaspoon ground white pepper**

12 **large (2-inch diameter) Campari tomatoes *or* 6 plum tomatoes**

Paprika

1 For potato salad, place potatoes in medium saucepan; cover with cold water. Bring to a boil over medium-high heat. Reduce heat; simmer 6 minutes or until potatoes are tender. Drain and place in medium bowl. Sprinkle with 2 tablespoons vinegar; stir gently to mix. Cool slightly.

2 Gently stir in mayonnaise, 2 tablespoons parsley, garlic, salt and white pepper. Cover and refrigerate about 2 hours or until cold.

3 Cut small slice from bottom of each tomato to allow tomatoes to stand upright. Cut top off each tomato; scoop out and discard pulp. Sprinkle remaining 1 tablespoon vinegar evenly into each tomato.

4 Fill each tomato with 2 to 3 tablespoons potato salad. Arrange tomatoes on serving plate; sprinkle with paprika and additional parsley. Serve immediately.

THICK POTATO CHIPS *with* BEER KETCHUP

Makes 4 servings

Beer Ketchup (recipe follows)

1 **quart peanut oil**

3 **baking potatoes**

Sea salt and black pepper

1 Prepare Beer Ketchup. Heat oil in large deep saucepan or Dutch oven to 345°F.

2 Cut potatoes into ¼-inch-thick slices. Fry in batches 2 minutes per side, turning to brown evenly on both sides. Drain on paper towels and immediately sprinkle with salt and pepper.

3 Serve with Beer Ketchup.

TIP: If the potatoes begin browning too quickly, turn down the heat and wait for the oil to cool to the proper temperature. Too high a temperature will not cook the potatoes completely, and too low a temperature will make the chips soggy.

BEER KETCHUP

Makes about 1 cup

¾ **cup ketchup**

¼ **cup beer**

1 **tablespoon Worcestershire sauce or soy sauce**

¼ **teaspoon onion powder**

Ground red pepper

1 Combine ketchup, beer, Worcestershire sauce, onion powder and red pepper in small saucepan. Bring to a boil. Reduce heat; simmer 2 to 3 minutes.

2 Remove from heat and let cool. Cover and store in refrigerator until ready to use.

BREADED GREEN BEANS

Makes 6 servings

1 **egg**

1 **pound green beans, ends trimmed**

½ **cup dry bread crumbs**

¼ **cup grated Parmesan cheese**

1 **tablespoon olive oil**

½ **teaspoon garlic powder**

¼ **teaspoon salt**

Ranch dressing (optional)

1 Preheat oven to 425°F. Line large baking sheet with parchment paper.

2 Whisk egg in large bowl. Add green beans; toss to coat. Combine bread crumbs, Parmesan cheese, oil, garlic powder and salt in small bowl. Sprinkle bread crumb mixture over green beans; toss to coat. Spread green beans on prepared baking sheet in single layer.

3 Bake 12 minutes; turn green beans. Bake 10 minutes or until crispy. Serve with ranch dressing, if desired.

BREADS

DATE-NUT BANANA BRAID

Makes 1 loaf

⅓ **cup milk**

2 **tablespoons butter**

3 **cups bread flour, divided**

¼ **cup plus 1 tablespoon sugar, divided**

1 **package (¼ ounce) rapid-rise active dry yeast**

¾ **teaspoon salt**

½ **cup mashed ripe banana (about 1 large)**

1 **egg, beaten**

½ **cup chopped pitted dates**

½ **cup chopped walnuts**

1 Combine milk and butter in small saucepan; heat to 130°F. Whisk 1 cup flour, ¼ cup sugar, yeast and salt in large bowl of electric stand mixer. Add milk mixture, banana and egg; beat at medium speed 3 minutes with paddle attachment.

2 Replace paddle attachment with dough hook; beat in dates, walnuts and enough remaining flour to form soft dough. Knead at medium-low speed 6 to 8 minutes or until dough is smooth and elastic. Place dough in greased bowl; turn to grease top. Cover and let rise in warm place about 30 minutes or until doubled in size.

3 Line baking sheet with parchment paper. Punch down dough. Divide dough into three pieces; roll each piece into 14-inch rope on lightly floured surface. Place ropes on prepared baking sheet; braid ropes and pinch ends to seal. Cover and let rise in warm place about 40 minutes or until doubled in size. Preheat oven to 375°F.

4 Sprinkle loaf with remaining 1 tablespoon sugar. Bake about 30 minutes or until golden brown and internal temperature reaches 200°F. Remove to wire rack; cool completely.

BREAD BOWLS
Makes 4 bread bowls

- **4 cups bread flour, divided**
- **¼ cup white cornmeal, plus additional for baking sheet**
- **1 package (¼ ounce) rapid-rise active dry yeast**
- **2 teaspoons sugar**
- **1½ teaspoons salt**
- **1⅓ cups warm water (120°F)**

1 Whisk 1 cup flour, ¼ cup cornmeal, yeast, sugar and salt in large bowl of electric stand mixer. Add warm water; beat at medium speed 2 minutes with paddle attachment.

2 Replace paddle attachment with dough hook; beat in enough remaining flour until firm dough forms. Knead at medium-low speed 5 minutes or until smooth and elastic. Shape dough into a ball. Place in large greased bowl; turn to grease top. Cover and let rise in warm place about 30 minutes or until doubled in size.

3 Line large baking sheet with parchment paper; sprinkle with cornmeal. Turn out dough onto lightly floured surface; punch down dough. Divide dough into four pieces; shape into round balls. Place on prepared baking sheet. Cover and let rise in warm place about 30 minutes or until doubled in size. Preheat oven to 425°F.

4 Bake 20 to 30 minutes. For a crisper crust, spray loaves with cold water several times during first 10 minutes of baking. Remove to wire rack; cool completely.

5 To make bread bowls, cut thin slice from top of each loaf. Remove inside of bread, leaving ½-inch shell on bottom and sides of loaves. (Reserve inside bread for another use.) If desired, bake bowls in 300°F oven 10 minutes to dry out bread slightly.

THREE-GRAIN BREAD
Makes 1 loaf

1 **cup whole wheat flour**

¾ **cup all-purpose flour, plus additional for dusting**

1 **package (¼ ounce) rapid-rise active dry yeast**

1 **cup milk**

1 **tablespoon olive oil**

2 **tablespoons honey**

1 **teaspoon salt**

½ **cup plus 1 tablespoon old-fashioned oats, divided**

¼ **cup whole grain cornmeal**

1 **egg beaten with 1 tablespoon water**

1 Combine whole wheat flour, all-purpose flour and yeast in large bowl.

2 Combine milk, oil, honey and salt in small saucepan; heat over low heat until warm (110° to 120°F). Stir into flour mixture; beat 3 minutes with electric mixer at high speed. Mix in ½ cup oats and cornmeal at low speed. If dough is too wet, add additional flour by teaspoonfuls until it begins to come together.

3 Replace paddle attachment with dough hook; knead on medium-low speed 5 minutes or until dough forms a ball. To knead by hand, place dough on floured surface and knead 8 minutes or until dough is smooth and elastic. Place dough in large greased bowl; turn to grease top. Cover and let rise in warm place about 1 hour or until dough is puffy and does not spring back when touched.

4 Punch dough down and shape into 8-inch long loaf. Place on baking sheet lightly dusted with cornmeal. Cover and let rise in warm place 45 minutes or until almost doubled in size.

5 Preheat oven to 375°F. Make shallow slash down center of loaf with sharp knife. Brush lightly with egg mixture and sprinkle with remaining 1 tablespoon oats. Bake 30 minutes or until loaf sounds hollow when tapped (200°F). Remove to wire rack; cool completely.

ANADAMA BREAD

Makes 2 loaves

2 **cups water**

½ **cup yellow cornmeal**

4 **tablespoons butter, cut into pieces**

½ **cup molasses**

5½ **to 6 cups all-purpose flour, divided**

1 **package (¼ ounce) active dry yeast**

1 **teaspoon salt**

1 Bring water to a boil in medium saucepan. Whisk in cornmeal; cook 1 minute, whisking constantly. Reduce heat to low; whisk in butter. Cook 3 minutes, stirring frequently. Stir in molasses. Transfer mixture to bowl of electric stand mixer; let stand 15 to 20 minutes to cool (about 90°F). Attach flat beater; stir in 2 cups flour, yeast and salt at low speed until rough dough forms.

2 Attach dough hook to mixer. Knead 5 to 7 minutes at low speed, adding remaining flour, ½ cup at a time until dough cleans sides of mixer bowl.

3 Shape dough into a ball. Place in large greased bowl; turn to grease top. Cover and let rise in warm place about 1 hour or until doubled in size.

4 Turn out dough onto lightly floured surface; knead 1 minute. Cut dough in half. Cover and let rest 10 minutes.

5 Grease two 9×5-inch loaf pans. Shape dough into loaves and place in pans. Cover and let rise in warm place about 30 minutes or until doubled in size.

6 Preheat oven to 350°F. Bake 30 to 35 minutes or until loaves are browned and sound hollow when tapped. Immediately remove from pans; cool completely on wire racks.

BLUEBERRY BREAD

Makes 1 loaf

2 cups all-purpose flour

¾ cup packed brown sugar

2 teaspoons baking powder

1 teaspoon baking soda

1 teaspoon salt

½ teaspoon ground nutmeg

¾ cup buttermilk*

1 egg

3 tablespoons oil or melted butter

1 cup fresh blueberries

*If you don't have buttermilk, combine ¾ cup milk and 1 teaspoon white vinegar or lemon juice in small bowl; let stand 5 minutes.

1 Preheat oven to 350°F. Spray 8½×4½-inch loaf pan with nonstick cooking spray.

2 Whisk flour, brown sugar, baking powder, baking soda, salt and nutmeg in large bowl. Whisk buttermilk, egg and oil in medium bowl; stir into flour mixture just until dry ingredients are moistened (batter should be lumpy). Fold in blueberries. Spread in prepared pan.

3 Bake 50 to 60 minutes or until toothpick inserted into center comes out clean. Cool in pan on wire rack 15 minutes. Remove from pan; cool completely on wire rack.

CRUNCHY WHOLE GRAIN BREAD

Makes 2 loaves

2 **cups warm water (105° to 115°F), divided**

⅓ **cup honey**

2 **tablespoons vegetable oil**

1 **tablespoon salt**

2 **packages (¼ ounce each) active dry yeast**

2 **to 2½ cups whole wheat flour, divided**

1 **cup bread flour**

1¼ **cups quick oats, divided**

½ **cup sunflower kernels**

½ **cup assorted grains and seeds***

1 **egg white**

1 **tablespoon water**

*Try a combination of uncooked millet, barley, chia seeds, flaxseed and pumpkin seeds.

1 Combine 1½ cups warm water, honey, oil and salt in small saucepan. Cook and stir over low heat until warm (115° to 120°F).

2 Dissolve yeast in remaining ½ cup warm water in large bowl of electric stand mixer. Let stand 5 minutes. Stir in honey mixture. Add 1 cup whole wheat flour and bread flour; knead with dough hook at low speed 2 minutes or until combined. Gradually stir in 1 cup oats, sunflower kernels and assorted grains. Add remaining whole wheat flour, ½ cup at a time, just until dough begins to form a ball. Continue kneading 7 to 10 minutes or until dough is smooth and elastic.

3 Place dough in large greased bowl; turn to grease top. Cover loosely with plastic wrap. Let rise in warm place 1½ to 2 hours or until doubled in size.

4 Grease two 9×5-inch loaf pans. Punch down dough. Divide in half. Shape each half into loaf; place in prepared pans. Cover and let rise in warm place 1 hour or until almost doubled in size.

5 Preheat oven to 375°F. Whisk egg white and water in small bowl. Brush tops of loaves with egg mixture. Sprinkle with remaining ¼ cup oats. Bake 35 to 45 minutes or until loaves sound hollow when tapped. Cool in pans 10 minutes. Remove to wire rack; cool completely.

FARMER-STYLE SOUR CREAM BREAD

Makes 1 loaf

1 cup sour cream

3 tablespoons water

2½ to 3 cups all-purpose flour, divided

1 package (¼ ounce) rapid-rise active dry yeast

2 tablespoons sugar

1½ teaspoons salt

¼ teaspoon baking soda

Vegetable oil

1 tablespoon sesame or poppy seeds

1 Combine sour cream and water in small saucepan. Heat over low heat until temperature reaches 120° to 130°F, stirring frequently. *Do not boil.*

2 Combine 2 cups flour, yeast, sugar, salt and baking soda in large bowl. Stir in sour cream mixture until well blended. Turn out dough onto lightly floured surface. Knead about 5 minutes, adding enough remaining flour until dough is smooth and elastic.

3 Grease large baking sheet. Shape dough into a ball; place on prepared baking sheet. Flatten into 8-inch circle. Brush top with oil; sprinkle with sesame seeds. Invert large bowl over dough and let rise in warm place 1 hour or until doubled in size.

4 Preheat oven to 350°F. Bake 22 to 27 minutes or until golden brown. Immediately remove to wire rack; cool completely.

TREACLE BREAD (BROWN SODA BREAD)

Makes 6 to 8 servings

2 cups all-purpose flour

1 cup whole wheat flour

1 teaspoon baking soda

½ teaspoon salt

½ teaspoon ground ginger

1¼ cups buttermilk, plus additional as needed

3 tablespoons dark molasses (preferably blackstrap)

1 Preheat oven to 375°F. Line baking sheet with parchment paper.

2 Whisk all-purpose flour, whole wheat flour, baking soda, salt and ginger in large bowl. Whisk 1¼ cups buttermilk and molasses in small bowl; stir into flour mixture just until dry ingredients are moistened. Add additional buttermilk by tablespoonfuls if needed to make dry, rough dough.

3 Turn out dough onto floured surface; knead 8 to 10 times or just until smooth. *Do not overknead.* Shape dough into round loaf about 1½ inches thick. Place on prepared baking sheet.

4 Use floured knife to cut halfway through dough, scoring into quarters. Sprinkle top of dough with additional flour, if desired.

5 Bake about 35 minutes or until bread sounds hollow when tapped. Remove to wire rack; cool slightly. Serve warm.

WALNUT FIG BREAD

Makes 1 loaf

2¼ **cups all-purpose flour, divided**

1 **cup whole wheat flour**

1 **package (¼ ounce) rapid-rise active dry yeast**

1 **tablespoon whole fennel seeds**

1½ **teaspoons salt**

1 **cup honey beer, milk or water**

2 **tablespoons butter**

1 **tablespoon honey**

1 **egg**

1 **cup chopped dried figs**

½ **cup chopped walnuts, toasted**

1 Combine 1 cup all-purpose flour, whole wheat flour, yeast, fennel seeds and salt in large bowl of electric stand mixer.

2 Combine beer, butter and honey in small saucepan; heat to 120°F. Add to dry ingredients; mix at low speed with paddle attachment until moistened. Add egg; beat until smooth. Add enough remaining flour to form soft dough. Stir in figs and walnuts.

3 Replace paddle attachment with dough hook. Knead at low speed 5 to 7 minutes or until dough is smooth and elastic. Shape dough into a ball. Place in large greased bowl; turn to grease top. Cover and let rise in warm place 1 hour or until doubled in size.

4 Punch dough down. Shape into round loaf; place on greased baking sheet. Cover and let rise in warm place 40 minutes.

5 Preheat oven to 350°F. Bake 30 to 35 minutes or until top is browned and loaf sounds hollow when tapped. Cool completely on wire rack.

TIP: To knead dough by hand, in step 3 turn dough out onto lightly floured surface; knead 5 to 6 minutes or until smooth and elastic.

ZUCCHINI BREAD

Makes 1 loaf

2½ **cups all-purpose flour**

⅔ **cup packed brown sugar**

⅓ **cup granulated sugar**

1 **tablespoon baking powder**

2 **teaspoons ground cinnamon**

1 **teaspoon baking soda**

1 **teaspoon salt**

¼ **teaspoon ground allspice**

¼ **teaspoon ground nutmeg**

¼ **teaspoon ground cardamom**

1¼ **cups whole milk**

2 **eggs**

¼ **cup canola oil**

1 **teaspoon vanilla**

1½ **cups grated zucchini,
    squeezed dry**

1 Preheat oven to 350°F. Grease 9×5-inch loaf pan.

2 Combine flour, brown sugar, granulated sugar, baking powder, cinnamon, baking soda, salt, allspice, nutmeg and cardamom in large bowl; mix well.

3 Whisk milk, eggs, oil and vanilla in medium bowl until well blended. Make well in flour mixture; pour in milk mixture and stir just until blended. Stir in zucchini. Pour into prepared pan.

4 Bake 1 hour or until toothpick inserted into center comes out almost clean. Cool in pan on wire rack 5 minutes. Remove to wire rack; cool completely.

PECAN PEACH MUFFINS

Makes 12 muffins

PECAN TOPPING

- ½ **cup chopped pecans**
- ⅓ **cup packed brown sugar**
- ¼ **cup all-purpose flour**
- 1 **teaspoon ground cinnamon**
- 2 **tablespoons melted butter**

MUFFINS

- 1½ **cups all-purpose flour**
- ½ **cup granulated sugar**
- 2 **teaspoons baking powder**
- 1 **teaspoon ground cinnamon**
- ¼ **teaspoon salt**
- ½ **cup (1 stick) butter, melted and cooled**
- ¼ **cup milk**
- 1 **egg**
- 2 **peaches, peeled and diced (about 1 cup)**

1 Preheat oven to 400°F. Line 12 standard (2½-inch) muffin cups with paper baking cups.

2 For topping, combine pecans, brown sugar, ¼ cup all-purpose flour and 1 teaspoon ground cinnamon in small bowl. Add 2 tablespoons butter; stir until mixture is crumbly.

3 For muffins, combine 1½ cups flour, granulated sugar, baking powder, 1 teaspoon cinnamon and salt in large bowl.

4 Whisk ½ cup butter, milk and egg in small bowl until blended. Stir into flour mixture just until moistened. Fold in peaches. Spoon evenly into prepared muffin cups. Sprinkle with topping.

5 Bake 18 to 20 minutes or until toothpick inserted into centers comes out clean. Remove to wire rack; cool completely.

DESSERTS

STRAWBERRY RHUBARB PIE
Makes 8 servings

Double-Crust Pie Pastry (recipe follows)

1½ **cups sugar**

½ **cup cornstarch**

2 **tablespoons quick-cooking tapioca**

1 **tablespoon grated lemon peel**

¼ **teaspoon ground allspice**

4 **cups sliced rhubarb (1-inch pieces)**

3 **cups sliced fresh strawberries**

1 **egg, lightly beaten**

1 Preheat oven to 425°F. Prepare pie pastry. Roll out one pastry disc into 11-inch circle on floured surface. Line 9-inch pie plate with pastry.

2 Combine sugar, cornstarch, tapioca, lemon peel and allspice in large bowl. Add rhubarb and strawberries; toss to coat. Pour into crust.

3 Roll out remaining pastry disc into 10-inch circle; cut into ½-inch-wide strips. Arrange in lattice design over fruit. Seal and flute edge. Brush pastry with beaten egg.

4 Bake 50 minutes or until filling is thick and bubbly and crust is golden brown. Cool on wire rack. Serve warm or at room temperature.

DOUBLE-CRUST PIE PASTRY:
Combine 2½ cups all-purpose flour, 1 teaspoon salt and 1 teaspoon sugar in large bowl. Cut in 1 cup (2 sticks) cubed unsalted butter with pastry blender or fingertips until mixture resembles coarse crumbs. Combine ⅓ cup ice water and 1 tablespoon cider vinegar in small bowl. Drizzle water mixture over flour mixture, 2 tablespoons at a time, stirring just until dough comes together. Divide dough in half. Shape each half into a disc; wrap in plastic wrap. Refrigerate 30 minutes.

FRESH CORN ICE CREAM
Makes about 1 pint

- **1 medium ear corn**
- **1 cup whole milk, plus more if necessary**
- **2 cups half-and-half**
- **¼ cup granulated sugar**
- **¼ cup packed brown sugar**
- **2 egg yolks**
- **¼ teaspoon vanilla**
- **¾ cup chopped salted pecans**

1 Scrape kernels from corn into medium saucepan. Add corncob and 1 cup milk. Partially cover and cook over very low heat 30 minutes. (If milk evaporates completely, add ¼ cup more.) Discard corncob.

2 Stir half-and-half, granulated sugar and brown sugar into corn mixture. Cook, uncovered, over low heat until sugar dissolves and liquid comes to a simmer, stirring frequently.

3 Whisk egg yolks in small bowl. Whisk ½ cup corn mixture into egg yolks in thin steady stream. Return mixture to saucepan. Cook over medium heat 10 minutes or until slightly thickened, stirring constantly. Remove from heat. Stir in vanilla.

4 Transfer to large bowl. Cover and refrigerate 4 to 6 hours or until cold.

5 Process corn mixture in ice cream maker according to manufacturer's directions. Add pecans during last 2 minutes of processing. Transfer to freezer container; press parchment paper directly onto surface. Cover and freeze 2 hours or until firm.

FRESH SUMMER FRUIT FOOL

Makes 4 servings

1 **cup sliced peeled fresh peaches (about 2 small)**

1 **cup sliced peeled fresh plums (about 2 large)**

1 **cup fresh raspberries**

8 **tablespoons powdered sugar, divided**

1 **tablespoon fresh lime juice**

1 **cup whipping cream**

   Grated lime peel (optional)

1 Place peaches, plums, raspberries, 6 tablespoons powdered sugar and lime juice in blender; blend until smooth. Cover and refrigerate at least 1 hour or up to 1 day.

2 Beat cream in medium bowl with electric mixer at high speed until soft peaks form. Add remaining 2 tablespoons powdered sugar; beat until stiff peaks form. Fold into fruit mixture. Spoon into four serving bowls; garnish with lime peel.

BLUEBERRY PIE
Makes 8 servings

Cream Cheese Pastry (recipe follows)

2 pints (4 cups) fresh blueberries

2 tablespoons cornstarch

⅔ cup blueberry preserves, melted

¼ teaspoon ground nutmeg

1 egg yolk

1 tablespoon milk

1 Preheat oven to 425°F. Prepare Cream Cheese Pastry. Roll out one disc of pastry into 11-inch circle on floured surface. Line 9-inch pie plate with pastry.

2 Combine blueberries and cornstarch in medium bowl; toss lightly to coat. Add preserves and nutmeg; mix lightly. Spoon into crust.

3 Roll out remaining disc of pastry into 11-inch circle; place over fruit mixture. Turn edge under; flute. Cut several slits in top crust to vent. If desired, cut decorative shapes from pastry scraps and place on top of pie. Bake 10 minutes.

4 *Reduce oven temperature to 350°F.* Combine egg yolk and milk in small bowl; brush lightly over crust. Bake 40 minutes or until crust is golden brown. Cool at least 15 minutes on wire rack. Serve warm, at room temperature or chilled.

CREAM CHEESE PASTRY
Makes pastry for one pie

1½ cups all-purpose flour

½ cup (1 stick) cold butter

3 ounces cold cream cheese, cubed

1 teaspoon vanilla

1 Place flour in large bowl. Cut in butter with pastry blender or fingertips until mixture resembles coarse crumbs. Cut in cream cheese and vanilla until mixture forms dough.

2 Divide dough in half. Shape each half into a disc; wrap in plastic wrap. Refrigerate 30 minutes.

RASPBERRY CLAFOUTIS

Makes 8 to 10 servings

3 **eggs**

⅓ **cup sugar**

1 **cup half-and-half**

2 **tablespoons butter, melted and slightly cooled**

½ **teaspoon vanilla**

⅔ **cup almond flour**

Pinch salt

12 **ounces fresh raspberries**

1 Preheat oven to 325°F. Generously grease 9-inch ceramic tart pan or pie plate.

2 Beat eggs and sugar in large bowl with electric mixer at medium speed 4 minutes or until slightly thickened. Add half-and-half, butter and vanilla; whisk to combine. Gradually whisk in almond flour and salt. Pour enough batter into prepared pan to just cover bottom. Bake 10 minutes or until set.

3 Remove pan from oven. Scatter raspberries evenly over baked batter. Stir remaining batter and pour over raspberries.

4 Bake 40 to 45 minutes or until center is set and top is golden. Cool completely on wire rack. Refrigerate leftovers.

NOTE: Clafoutis is a rustic French dish that is made by topping fresh fruit with a custard-like batter and baking. The most famous and traditional clafoutis is made with cherries, but berries, plums, peaches and pears are also used.

PLUM CAKE *with* STREUSEL TOPPING

Makes 6 servings

Streusel Topping (recipe follows)

1 **cup plus 2 tablespoons all-purpose flour**

½ **teaspoon baking powder**

¼ **teaspoon salt**

¼ **teaspoon baking soda**

6 **tablespoons (¾ stick) butter, softened**

¼ **cup granulated sugar**

¼ **cup packed brown sugar**

1 **teaspoon vanilla**

2 **eggs**

¼ **cup buttermilk**

3 **medium plums, pitted and cut into 8 wedges***

*Plums should be underripe and slightly soft to the touch.

1 Preheat oven to 350°F. Grease 9-inch springform pan. Line bottom of pan with parchment paper; grease paper. Prepare Streusel Topping.

2 Combine flour, baking powder, salt and baking soda in medium bowl.

3 Beat butter in large bowl with electric mixer at medium speed 1 minute. Add granulated sugar and brown sugar; beat 1 minute or until light and fluffy. Beat in vanilla. Add eggs, one at a time, beating well after each addition.

4 Alternately add flour mixture and buttermilk, beating well at low speed after each addition. Spread batter in prepared pan.

5 Arrange plum wedges around outer edge and in center of batter. Sprinkle with topping. Bake 30 minutes or until cake springs back when lightly touched.

6 Place cake on wire rack. Run thin knife or spatula around edge of pan. Remove side of pan; cool 20 minutes. Transfer cake to serving plate. Serve warm or at room temperature.

STREUSEL TOPPING: Combine ¼ cup all-purpose flour, 3 tablespoons packed brown sugar and ½ teaspoon ground cinnamon in medium bowl. Mix in 2 tablespoons softened butter with fingertips until flour mixture is crumbly.

FRESH NECTARINE PIE *with* STRAWBERRY TOPPING

Makes 8 servings

Pie Pastry for Single Crust Pie (page 159)

1½ **pounds nectarines, pitted and cut into ½-inch slices**

½ **cup sugar, divided**

1 **pint fresh strawberries, hulled**

1 **tablespoon fresh lemon juice**

1 **tablespoon cornstarch**

Whipped cream (optional)

1 Preheat oven to 425°F. Prepare pie pastry. Roll out pastry into 11-inch circle on lightly floured surface. Line 9-inch pie plate with pastry; trim and flute edge. Refrigerate until ready to fill.

2 Reserve 6 to 8 nectarine slices for garnish; chop remaining nectarines. Place nectarines in pie crust; sprinkle with 2 tablespoons sugar. Bake 30 minutes or until crust is browned and fruit is tender. Cool on wire rack 30 minutes.

3 Meanwhile, place strawberries in food processor; process until puréed. Press purée through fine-mesh sieve; discard seeds and pulp. Pour liquid into 1-cup measure; add lemon juice and enough water to equal 1 cup liquid.

4 Combine remaining 6 tablespoons sugar and cornstarch in small saucepan. Gradually add strawberry mixture; stir until sugar and cornstarch are dissolved. Bring to a boil over medium heat; cook and stir 5 minutes or until mixture boils and thickens. Remove from heat; cool 15 minutes.

5 Spread strawberry mixture over pie, completely covering nectarines. Cool completely. Refrigerate at least 2 hours or up to 8 hours; cover with plastic wrap after 1 hour. Top with whipped cream, if desired; garnish with reserved nectarine slices.

PIE PASTRY *for* SINGLE CRUST PIE
Makes pastry for one pie

1¼ **cups all-purpose flour**

¼ **teaspoon baking powder**

⅛ **teaspoon salt**

¼ **cup (½ stick) cold butter, cut into pieces**

3 **tablespoons ice water**

1 **teaspoon cider vinegar**

1 Combine flour, baking powder and salt in medium bowl. Cut in butter with pastry blender or fingertips until mixture resembles coarse crumbs. Combine ice water and vinegar in small bowl. Add water mixture to flour mixture by tablespoons until dough begins to form. Gather into a ball.

2 Shape dough into a disc. Wrap dough in plastic wrap; refrigerate at least 30 minutes.

PEACH *and* BLUEBERRY CRISP

Makes 4 servings

- 3 **cups fresh sliced peeled peaches**
- 1 **cup fresh blueberries**
- 2 **tablespoons granulated sugar**
- ¼ **teaspoon ground nutmeg**
- 2 **tablespoons old-fashioned oats**
- 2 **tablespoons crisp rice cereal**
- 2 **tablespoons all-purpose flour**
- 1 **tablespoon packed brown sugar**
- 1 **tablespoon butter, melted**
- ⅛ **teaspoon ground cinnamon**

1 Preheat oven to 375°F.

2 Combine peaches and blueberries in ungreased 8-inch round cake pan. Combine granulated sugar and nutmeg in small bowl. Sprinkle over fruit; toss gently to combine.

3 Combine oats, rice cereal, flour, brown sugar, butter and cinnamon in small bowl. Sprinkle over fruit.

4 Bake 35 to 40 minutes or until peaches are tender and topping is golden brown.

ZUCCHINI BASIL CUPCAKES
Makes 16 cupcakes

1¼ **cups all-purpose flour**

1½ **teaspoons baking powder**

1 **teaspoon baking soda**

½ **teaspoon salt**

1 **cup granulated sugar**

½ **cup vegetable oil**

2 **eggs**

½ **cup milk**

1 **cup grated zucchini, pressed or squeezed to remove liquid**

¼ **cup finely chopped fresh basil**

1 **package (8 ounces) cream cheese, softened**

¼ **cup (½ stick) butter, softened**

1¾ **cups powdered sugar**

1 **teaspoon vanilla**

1 Preheat oven to 350°F. Line 16 standard (2½-inch) muffin cups with paper baking cups.

2 Whisk flour, baking powder, baking soda and salt in small bowl. Whisk granulated sugar, oil and eggs in large bowl until well blended. Add flour mixture and milk; mix well. Stir in zucchini and basil. Spoon batter evenly into prepared muffin cups.

3 Bake 25 minutes or until toothpick inserted into centers comes out clean. Cool in pans 5 minutes. Remove to wire racks; cool completely.

4 For frosting, beat cream cheese and butter in large bowl with electric mixer at medium speed until well combined. Add powdered sugar and vanilla; beat at low speed 1 minute. Beat at medium-high speed 5 minutes or until fluffy. Pipe or spread frosting over cupcakes.

CARROT CAKE

Makes 10 to 12 servings

2 **cups granulated sugar**

1½ **cups vegetable oil**

1 **teaspoon vanilla**

2½ **cups all-purpose flour**

2 **tablespoons ground cinnamon, divided**

1 **teaspoon salt**

1 **teaspoon baking soda**

½ **teaspoon ground ginger**

4 **eggs, beaten**

2 **cups grated carrots**

1 **cup canned crushed pineapple, drained**

¾ **cup chopped pecans**

½ **cup golden raisins**

2 **cups pineapple juice**

Cream Cheese Frosting (recipe follows)

1 Preheat oven to 350°F. Grease and flour two 8-inch round cake pans.

2 Combine granulated sugar, oil and vanilla in large bowl. Whisk flour, 1 tablespoon cinnamon, salt, baking soda and ginger into medium bowl; add to sugar mixture alternately with eggs, stirring well after each addition. Stir in carrots, pineapple, pecans and raisins until well blended. Pour evenly into prepared pans.

3 Bake 45 to 50 minutes or until toothpick inserted into centers comes out clean. Poke holes in warm cake layers with wooden skewer. Pour 1 cup pineapple juice over each layer. Let layers stand in pans until cool and juice is absorbed.

4 Prepare Cream Cheese Frosting.

5 Invert one cake layer onto serving plate; frost top of cake. Place second cake layer on top of first cake layer. Frost top and side of cake. Sprinkle remaining 1 tablespoon cinnamon over frosting. Store cake in refrigerator.

CREAM CHEESE FROSTING

½ **cup (1 stick) butter, softened**

4 **ounces cream cheese, softened**

2 **tablespoons vanilla**

2 **cups powdered sugar**

Whipping cream or milk

1 Beat butter, cream cheese and vanilla in large bowl with electric mixer at medium speed until light and fluffy.

2 Beat in powdered sugar at low speed until well blended. If frosting is too thick, add cream, 1 tablespoon at a time, until desired consistency is reached.

SAUCES & PICKLES

SWEET FREEZER PICKLES
Makes about 6 cups

2 pounds unpeeled cucumbers (about 4 medium), sliced

½ red onion, sliced

1 red bell pepper, sliced

1 stalk celery, finely chopped

3 carrots, quartered lengthwise, then cut into 3-inch pieces

¾ cup sugar

¾ cup cider vinegar

2 teaspoons mustard seeds *or* ¼ teaspoon red pepper flakes

1 teaspoon salt

1 Combine cucumbers, onion, bell pepper, celery and carrots in 1-gallon resealable food storage bag. Whisk sugar, vinegar, mustard seeds and salt in medium bowl; pour over vegetables. Seal bag, releasing excess air. Freeze at least 24 hours.

2 Remove from freezer; thaw at room temperature. Pour into large bowl; cover with plastic wrap. Refrigerate 2 days. Transfer to jars with tight-fitting lids; store in refrigerator 3 weeks or freeze up to 1 year.

TIP: Serve as you would any other bread-and-butter pickle. These are great on sandwiches and with grilled chicken or ribs. To make relish, chop just before serving.

LEMON CURD

Makes 1¾ cups

½ **cup sugar**

6 **tablespoons butter**

⅓ **cup fresh lemon juice**

½ **tablespoon grated lemon peel**

Pinch of salt

2 **eggs, beaten**

1 Combine sugar, butter, lemon juice, lemon peel and salt in medium saucepan. Heat over medium heat, stirring until butter is melted and sugar is dissolved. Remove from heat.

2 Gradually whisk in eggs in thin steady stream. Cook over medium-low heat 5 minutes or until thickened to the consistency of pudding, whisking constantly.

3 Strain through fine-mesh sieve into medium bowl. Press plastic wrap onto surface; refrigerate until cold. Transfer to jar with tight-fitting lid or food storage container.

TIP: Try using Meyer lemons when they're available. Their flavor is more floral and less tart than regular lemons. Or try using clementines or blood oranges instead of the lemons.

RHUBARB CHUTNEY

Makes about 2 cups

1 cup coarsely chopped peeled apple

½ cup sugar

¼ cup water

¼ cup dark raisins

1 teaspoon grated lemon peel

2 cups sliced rhubarb (½-inch pieces)

3 tablespoons coarsely chopped pecans

2 to 3 teaspoons white vinegar

¾ teaspoon ground cinnamon (optional)

1 Combine apple, sugar, water, raisins and lemon peel in medium saucepan; cook over medium heat until sugar is dissolved, stirring constantly. Reduce heat to low; simmer about 5 minutes or until apple is almost tender.

2 Stir in rhubarb and pecans; bring to a boil over high heat. Reduce heat to low; simmer 8 to 10 minutes or until slightly thickened, stirring occasionally. Stir in vinegar and cinnamon, if desired, during last 2 to 3 minutes of cooking.

3 Remove from heat; cool to room temperature. Cover and refrigerate until ready to serve.

FRESH TOMATO SALSA

Makes about 1 1/2 cups

2 medium tomatoes, finely chopped

¼ cup finely chopped white onion

¼ cup coarsely chopped fresh cilantro

1 to 2 jalapeño peppers, seeded and minced

2 tablespoons fresh lime juice

¼ teaspoon salt

1 Combine tomatoes, onion, cilantro, jalapeños, lime juice and salt in medium bowl; mix well.

2 Let stand, covered, at room temperature 1 to 2 hours for flavors to blend.

172

QUICK PICKLED GREEN BEANS

Makes 3 ½ cups

½ **pound whole green beans (3½ cups loosely packed)**

½ **red bell pepper, cut into strips (optional)**

1 **jalapeño or other hot pepper, sliced**

1 **clove garlic, cut in half**

1 **bay leaf**

1 **cup white wine vinegar**

1 **cup water**

½ **cup dry white wine**

1 **tablespoon sugar**

1 **tablespoon salt**

1 **tablespoon whole coriander seeds**

1 **tablespoon mustard seeds**

1 **tablespoon whole peppercorns**

1 Wash beans; trim stem ends, if desired. Place in glass dish just large enough to hold beans and 2½ cups liquid. Add bell pepper strips, if desired. Tuck jalapeño slices, garlic and bay leaf among beans.

2 Combine vinegar, water, wine, sugar, salt, coriander seeds, mustard seeds and peppercorns in medium saucepan. Bring to a boil, stirring until sugar and salt are dissolved. Reduce heat; simmer 5 minutes.

3 Pour mixture over beans, making sure beans are fully submerged in liquid. Add additional hot water to cover, if necessary. Cover and refrigerate at least 24 hours.

4 Drain beans. Remove and discard bay leaf.

SPICED APPLE BUTTER

Makes 2 cups

**2 pounds Granny Smith or any
tart apples, peeled, cored
and chopped (about
6½ cups)**

1 cup apple cider

**½ cup packed dark brown
sugar**

1 tablespoon fresh lemon juice

½ teaspoon ground cinnamon

⅛ teaspoon ground ginger

⅛ teaspoon ground cloves

1 Combine apples and cider in large saucepan. Bring to a boil over medium heat. Reduce heat; simmer 30 minutes or until apples are very tender.

2 Purée apple mixture in batches in blender, returning blended apple mixture to saucepan after each batch. (Or use immersion blender.)

3 Add brown sugar, lemon juice, cinnamon, ginger and cloves to apple mixture. Bring to a boil over medium heat. Reduce heat; simmer 25 minutes or until thickened, stirring and scraping bottom and side of saucepan frequently. Cool completely. Store in airtight container in refrigerator up to 1 month.

GINGERED APPLE CRANBERRY CHUTNEY

Makes about 3 cups

2 medium Granny Smith apples, peeled and diced

1 package (12 ounces) fresh or thawed frozen cranberries

1¼ cups packed brown sugar

¾ cup cranberry juice

½ cup golden raisins

¼ cup chopped crystallized ginger

¼ cup cider vinegar

1 teaspoon ground cinnamon

⅛ teaspoon ground allspice

1 Combine apples, cranberries, brown sugar, cranberry juice, raisins, ginger, vinegar, cinnamon and allspice in medium saucepan. Bring to a boil over high heat. Reduce heat to medium; simmer 20 to 25 minutes or until mixture is very thick, stirring occasionally.

2 Remove from heat; cool completely. Store in airtight container in refrigerator up to 2 weeks.

PESTO SAUCE

Makes ½ cup

- **1 cup packed fresh basil leaves**
- **½ cup pine nuts or almonds, toasted***
- **2 cloves garlic**
- **½ teaspoon salt**
- **¼ teaspoon black pepper**
- **¼ cup olive oil**
- **½ cup grated or shredded Parmesan cheese**

*To toast pine nuts, place in small nonstick skillet. Cook over medium-low heat about 5 minutes or until nuts begin to brown, stirring frequently.

1 Place basil, pine nuts, garlic, salt and pepper in food processor; pulse until coarsely chopped.

2 With motor running, drizzle in oil. Process about 30 seconds or until almost smooth. Stir in cheese. Transfer pesto to jar with tight-fitting lid; store in refrigerator or freeze for longer storage.

CRANBERRY-APPLE RELISH

Makes 2½ cups

1 cup sweet onion, chopped

1 cup granulated sugar

¾ cup unsweetened apple juice

½ cup packed brown sugar

1 teaspoon ground cinnamon

½ teaspoon ground ginger

⅛ teaspoon ground cloves

1 package (12 ounces) fresh or frozen cranberries

1 large Granny Smith apple, peeled and cut into ½-inch pieces

1 Combine onion, granulated sugar, juice, brown sugar, cinnamon, ginger and cloves in medium saucepan. Bring to a boil over high heat. Reduce heat; simmer 5 minutes.

2 Add cranberries and apple; simmer 20 minutes or until mixture is very thick, stirring occasionally.

3 Cool to room temperature. Transfer to serving dish or refrigerate until ready to serve.

PICKLED RED ONIONS
Makes about ½ cup

½ **cup thinly sliced red onion**

¼ **cup white wine vinegar**

2 **tablespoons water**

1 **teaspoon sugar**

½ **teaspoon salt**

Combine all ingredients in large glass jar. Seal jar; shake well. Refrigerate at least 1 hour or up to 1 week.

MANGO SALSA
Makes about 1 cup

1 **large ripe mango, peeled and cubed**

1 **jalapeño pepper, seeded and minced**

3 **tablespoons minced red onion**

3 **tablespoons fresh lime juice**

2 **tablespoons minced fresh cilantro or mint**

½ **teaspoon salt**

Combine mango, jalapeño, onion, lime juice, cilantro and salt in small bowl. Serve immediately or transfer to jar with tight-fitting lid and refrigerate.

PICKLED RED ONIONS

TOMATO SAUCE

Makes about 3 cups

5 **tablespoons butter**

1 **clove garlic, minced**

2 **cups peeled fresh tomatoes**

1 **can (8 ounces) tomato sauce**

¾ **teaspoon salt**

½ **teaspoon dried oregano**

½ **teaspoon dried basil**

½ **teaspoon dried rosemary, crushed**

⅛ **teaspoon black pepper**

1 Heat butter in large saucepan over medium heat until melted and bubbly. Add garlic; cook and stir 30 seconds. Press tomatoes with juice through sieve into garlic mixture; discard seeds. Stir in tomato sauce, salt, oregano, basil, rosemary and pepper.

2 Cover and simmer 30 minutes. Uncover and simmer 15 minutes more or until sauce thickens, stirring occasionally.

TIP: To easily peel tomatoes, cut an X in the stem end. Drop them in boiling water and cook about 30 seconds. Remove with tongs and peel off the skin when the tomatoes are cool enough to handle.

⇶ INDEX ⇇

METRIC CONVERSION CHART

VOLUME MEASUREMENTS (dry)

$\frac{1}{8}$ teaspoon = 0.5 mL
$\frac{1}{4}$ teaspoon = 1 mL
$\frac{1}{2}$ teaspoon = 2 mL
$\frac{3}{4}$ teaspoon = 4 mL
1 teaspoon = 5 mL
1 tablespoon = 15 mL
2 tablespoons = 30 mL
$\frac{1}{4}$ cup = 60 mL
$\frac{1}{3}$ cup = 75 mL
$\frac{1}{2}$ cup = 125 mL
$\frac{2}{3}$ cup = 150 mL
$\frac{3}{4}$ cup = 175 mL
1 cup = 250 mL
2 cups = 1 pint = 500 mL
3 cups = 750 mL
4 cups = 1 quart = 1 L

VOLUME MEASUREMENTS (fluid)

1 fluid ounce (2 tablespoons) = 30 mL
4 fluid ounces ($\frac{1}{2}$ cup) = 125 mL
8 fluid ounces (1 cup) = 250 mL
12 fluid ounces (1$\frac{1}{2}$ cups) = 375 mL
16 fluid ounces (2 cups) = 500 mL

WEIGHTS (mass)

$\frac{1}{2}$ ounce = 15 g
1 ounce = 30 g
3 ounces = 90 g
4 ounces = 120 g
8 ounces = 225 g
10 ounces = 285 g
12 ounces = 360 g
16 ounces = 1 pound = 450 g

DIMENSIONS

$\frac{1}{16}$ inch = 2 mm
$\frac{1}{8}$ inch = 3 mm
$\frac{1}{4}$ inch = 6 mm
$\frac{1}{2}$ inch = 1.5 cm
$\frac{3}{4}$ inch = 2 cm
1 inch = 2.5 cm

OVEN TEMPERATURES

250°F = 120°C
275°F = 140°C
300°F = 150°C
325°F = 160°C
350°F = 180°C
375°F = 190°C
400°F = 200°C
425°F = 220°C
450°F = 230°C

BAKING PAN SIZES

Utensil	Size in Inches/Quarts	Metric Volume	Size in Centimeters
Baking or Cake Pan (square or rectangular)	8×8×2	2 L	20×20×5
	9×9×2	2.5 L	23×23×5
	12×8×2	3 L	30×20×5
	13×9×2	3.5 L	33×23×5
Loaf Pan	8×4×3	1.5 L	20×10×7
	9×5×3	2 L	23×13×7
Round Layer Cake Pan	8×1½	1.2 L	20×4
	9×1½	1.5 L	23×4
Pie Plate	8×1¼	750 mL	20×3
	9×1¼	1 L	23×3
Baking Dish or Casserole	1 quart	1 L	—
	1½ quart	1.5 L	—
	2 quart	2 L	—